Fiction Writing 101:

A Home Study Course

(especially for homeschoolers)

By

Mike Dellosso

ISBN: **1536806951**

ISBN-13: **978-1536806953**

INTRODUCTION TO FICTION WRITING AND THIS BOOK

Stories are powerful things. They have the ability to enlighten people, enthrall them, convict, encourage, and move at the deepest levels of the soul. And the author who writes the story possesses a great amount of power. And a great amount of responsibility. We—authors—have the power to manipulate a reader's emotions, to roll them around in our hands as easily as a potter molds a lump of wet clay.

But fiction writing is not easy. It's an art and as with any art form it takes time and practice and dedication to improve it and become accomplished at it. I always chuckle when someone says to me, "I could write a book if I only had time." No, you couldn't. Not even with all the time in the world. Not now, anyway. No one expects to pick up a paint brush and create a work of art like Van Gogh in just a few sittings. No one expects to sit down at a piano and have her fingers know magically where to go on the keyboard. It takes work, effort, perspiration, tears, and hours upon hours of dedicated practice to master painting or piano playing. Fiction writing is no different.

You have to start somewhere and I hope this course will be a good beginning for you. A few things are assumed going into this course. One, that you have a basic grasp on grammar and punctuation. Two, that you love to read. Writing fiction well is all about reading. I've never met a painter who doesn't enjoy observing paintings or a pianist who doesn't enjoy listening to piano music. Three, that you are open to learning. A mind set on learning is like a sponge and you'll get so much more out of this book.

So how would I recommend using this book? I would suggest working through it from front to back. Make sure to read the additional readings posted for each section. They contain some really good information. Assignments are to be completed as you go but feel free to go back and revise writings as you learn more techniques.

Parents of homeschoolers, I would suggest waiting until the entire course is complete before grading your student's writing assignments. That way you're grading his or her best work and not a work-in-progress. Also, the course is designed to be a ½ high school credit but it can be counted as 1 credit depending on how much time your student puts into the writing assignments and if it is supplemented with at least five novels for the student to read on his or her own. I'll let you choose the novels since you know your child better than me.

*Please keep in mind that this is a beginner's fiction writing course. There is much more to be learned about fiction writing than can be covered in this course but this information will give any aspiring writer a great foundation to build on.

There is some good information in the appendix as well. Don't forget that.

**The final project for this course, located at the end of the book, is to write a 5,000 word short story using the skills and techniques you learn in this course. Think carefully about this project. Put your best foot forward. Be creative. I've included a sample short story for you to read.

Parents and students, if you have questions, please feel free to email me at

mikedellosso6797@gmail.com.

CHARACTERS

Draw from your own experience

There's a writing mantra that says "Write what you know." I'm not a hundred percent behind that but it does have some validity when it comes to creating characters. In order for readers to become personally involved in your story's characters those characters have to feel authentic. In general, we humans are pretty good judges of character. Yes, there are those who are just naïve or gullible or choose not to see reality and get duped by every and any fraud who comes along. But mostly, we can tell if someone is real or not, if he or she is authentic. We're pretty good at recognizing the masks we all wear.

The same is true for your fictional characters. They have to seem real; the reader has to picture them as not fictional at all. So what's the secret? How do you create characters who walk right off the page and into your reader's life? You make them authentic. And how do you do that? You tap into your own soul, heart, mind . . . you write what you know: Yourself.

Fiction writing is about being vulnerable, it's about being transparent and humble and genuine. Fiction writers expose themselves. We stand in front of a crowd and say, "This is who I am with all the scars, warts, wrinkles, folds, and blemishes that go along with me."

And you know what? Readers say, "Yes! That's me, too."

To create authentic characters look inside yourself. Tap into your heart and soul, explore the darkness there, the wounds, the hurts, the regrets and resentments. Bask in the light, the victories, the celebrations. Feel the emotions all over again. Contemplate them. The more real they become to you again the more genuinely you will describe them as they relate to your characters.

We all have experiences we can tap into. Maybe you were bullied. Or lost a loved one. Maybe your parents got divorced. Or you were abused. Maybe you have some disability. Physical. Mental. Emotional. We've all fought battles and have wounds. And we've all had moments of great joy, ecstasy, triumph. Some great accomplishment. Something we are beyond grateful and thankful for.

These are the emotions of life, the struggles, the victories, the pain and the healing. Fiction writers need to learn to explore those emotions, to dig them up no matter how painful and relive them so our characters can live them and our readers can understand what it's like.

This is your challenge. Be vulnerable. Be real. Think. Explore. Share. We're not just in the business of writing stories, our task is to take the reader there, show them so they will know.

Now, I know what you're thinking. But what if I want to put my character through something that I've never been through? Great thought. Really. And there's a couple different ways to deal with that.

One, do some homework. Talk to someone who has gone through it, or read first-hand accounts of folks who have experienced it. Let's say you want your main character to being going through her parents' divorce. But your parents are still happily married. How do you understand divorce? How do you get to that place and experience it? We all know folks who have been through divorce. If they are willing to share their experience, talk to them. Don't "interview" them just talk to them, ask them questions, seek to learn and understand, not interrogate. Or, if you don't feel comfortable doing that or don't know anyone willing to talk about it, do some research. Read a book on dealing with divorce, experiencing it. Do what you can to understand the mechanics of it, the process, the nuts and bolts. As best you can, understand the emotions involved.

Two, tap into the basic emotions involved. We all experience the same sets of emotions. Hurt, abandonment, anger, frustration, confusion, and the list goes on. The situations may change, the settings may change, the people may change. But the emotions are much the same. Once you have at least a solid understanding of the framework and process of the situation your character will be going through, then overlay your own experience with the emotions involved in that situation.

So let's take our example of divorce. My parents are not divorced. I have no idea what it's like as a child to go through divorce. But I've talked to enough people and read enough accounts to understand the process and the emotional stress of it. There's a sense of hurt, abandonment, confusion. There's guilt. There's a longing for things to return to the way they were. I know what those emotions feel like. I know what it's like to be hurt, to feel abandoned, confused. I know how guilt stings and gnaws and aches. I've experienced that longing for "the way things were." Not in the context of divorce mind you, but emotions are emotions. And I'm all-too-familiar with emotions. So I can take the emotions I've experience and know well and insert them into the context of divorce. It is real? No, it's fiction. But to the reader it feels real.

Real people have flaws, quirks, and are interesting

When you're creating characters don't forget to give them flaws. We are all flawed people. There is no one who is perfect! Readers want to be able to identify with fictional characters and flaws allow them to identify. For help with this, tap into your own flaws. You know how they feel, the wrestling match you go through every day with them. You know how it feels to struggle with those flaws, the guilt you feel when you give into them, and the joy when you conquer them. The reader won't know how personal you're getting but it will allow you to express that flaw in a very genuine, realistic way.

For instance, I wrestle with my faith on a regular basis. I struggle to stay close to God. I question Him. I doubt Him at times. So many of the lead characters in my books struggle with the same thing. And most people do! Readers can identify, they can say, "Yeah, I know what that's like and how that feels."

Or how about a short temper or a problem with lying or wandering eyes? What's your flaw? Or what's at least a flaw you can identify with personally? Tap into it. Make it a part of your character's biographical sketch. The more real and genuine you can make your characters the more the reader will be able to identify with him or her. And readers who identify with characters are readers who continue to read and enjoy a story.

Protagonists people care about

A word about protagonists. Readers want a protagonist they can route for. They want to care about the person, care about what motivates him or her. They want to identify with her and care about what she cares about. When creating your protagonist keep all this in mind. You're looking for someone who is flawed and up against incredible odds. Someone who wants to do the right thing but struggles to do it. Someone the reader can say, "If she was a real person I'd want to be her friend."

Notice in the first chapter of *Fear Mountain* how the main character, Billy Harding, is introduced. The reader finds out some important information about him almost immediately and a bond is formed with the reader.

> From the moment I peeled open my eyes against the thick darkness I knew I would not soon forget this night.
> I don't claim to have any paranormal abilities, no premonitory visions, no mind-reading skills. I don't tinker with Tarot cards, can't gaze into a crystal ball and portend the future.

And I only have five senses.

But somehow I just *knew*.

As I lay in my cot, wool blanket pulled to my nose, burrowed into the warmth it provided, an unsettled feeling seeped into my belly and lingered like an unwanted guest. Something wasn't right. I reached up with both hands and rubbed the grit from my eyes, the sleep cobwebs from my lids. Opening my eyes the rest of the way, I saw only darkness. I could hear my brother, just feet to my left, in a low, steady snore. I listened for the familiar rhythm of Dad's deep breathing, like a bear in hibernation, but didn't hear it. Didn't hear Pop either.

We were on the annual hunting trip to the north woods and at seventeen, it was my first trip, my first tag-along into the wild outdoors, a place where I reckoned humans were as unwelcome as lions at a wildebeest reunion.

I'm no hunter. Killing doesn't come naturally for me. It's not that I think there's anything fundamentally or morally wrong with killing for meat, I just don't have the stomach for it. And besides, I'm not the outdoors type.

I'm a disappointment.

But as I lay there, awakened in the middle of the first night of our four-day trip, listening to the deep silence broken only by Henry's even snore, I knew—*knew*—something was wrong. Call it intuition or extrasensory perception—I call it God's voice, that still small whisper that speaks, not to the ears, but to the heart—but the absence of Dad's bear-like respirations and Pop's low, bronchial rumble told me I needed to get up and brave the chilly night air.

And I dreaded it. As I said, I'm no outdoorsmen. I prefer to spend my time in the comfort of a home, reading and filling my head with Bible stories, words of wisdom and comfort from bygone theologians, and facts about the natural world, God's creation, His handiwork. My hands are soft, supple, my muscles mostly undeveloped. My lungs are weak. I'm not at all suited for tramping about the woods in the middle of the night. But, if pressed—and pressed hard, mind you—I will do what needs to be done, when it needs to be done.

I pushed back the blanket, swung my legs over the edge of the cot, and sat, breathed in the coolness. Two days prior, a cold front had moved down from Canada, ambushing most of the northeast with unseasonably cool weather. The fire in the wood stove had died and a chill hung in the air like a bitter phantom, a gift from our northerly Canuck neighbors.

For a minute, I sat still, listening, trying to clear my mind of the fog that sleep had left. The cabin windows were cloaked in black, as if someone had sneaked outside and draped velvet curtains over them. The lack of light, even moonlight, and the absence of birdsong, said it was early morning. Mid-September, the moon bids farewell to the mid-Maine night sky and tucks itself into a shadowy sleepiness around the midnight hour. Maybe Dad and Pop went outside to empty their bladders. Maybe only Pop had to respond to nature's urgings and Dad went with him. Pop's bladder wasn't what it used it be. I pictured Dad standing, thick arms crossed, hair mussed and wild, eyes half-closed with his back to his father while Pop did his best to bypass his enlarged prostate and water a young sapling.

I listened again and tried to pick out the sound of footsteps in leaves or the low broken hiss of a whisper. But heard neither. The only sound was the continuous, almost hypnotic rhythm of Henry's sleep.

Running a hand over my jaw, feeling the soft, patchy bristles from a day's worth of growth, I slid my feet into the slippers waiting on the floor. I reached down and grabbed the flashlight, a trusty Lightmaster lantern, and stood; my knees and ankles cracked in protest.

Leaving the light off, I shuffled over to Henry's cot and knelt beside it.

I shook his shoulder and whispered, "Henry, wake up. Henry."

My brother grumbled and snorted—sounds that would have been more at home in a bear's den than in a civilized cabin— pushed my hand away in his sleep, and tried to roll over. I gripped his shoulder and pulled him back to face me. "Henry. C'mon, wake up." I said it in a small voice, not loud but louder than a whisper.

Henry stirred again, shrugged off my hand and mumbled something unintelligible as if sometime during his stopover in REM sleep his tongue had swollen to fill his mouth.

I shook him again. "Henry, wake up. C'mon. Dad's gone. So is Pop."

Henry grunted and rolled onto his back. In the darkness I felt his hands lift to his face. "What? Billy, what're you doin'?" His voice was thick and raspy, stale from sleep.

I hit the flashlight's toggle switch and immediately blinded Henry with the brilliance of the bulb. Like a funnel weaver spider retreating into the dark recesses of his lair, he jerked back and shrunk beneath the cover of his wool blanket. "Billy, get that thing outta my face!"

"Sorry." I redirected the beam of light to the wall.

Henry poked his head out from the covers. His hair was matted flat on one side of his head; his eyes were puffy with sleep. He grimaced and ran a hand through his hair. "Well, what's the time?"

I slid my watch under the flashlight's beam. "Two-forty."

Henry propped himself on one elbow and motioned for the light. I handed it to him, and he promptly aimed it at my eyes.

"Hey!" I shielded my face. "Knock it off."

"See how you like it."

He swept the beam around the small cabin. The rough-hewn table and four chairs sat undisturbed as we had left them before retiring for the night. The wood stove squatted quietly in the corner, radiating only a faint memory of heat. Our guns waited patiently in the corner, no doubt itching to do what they do best. And on the far side of the cabin, Dad's bunk lay empty, as did Pop's. Covers ruffled and pulled back, pillow still indented with the impression of his head, Dad's looked like he'd left in a hurry. Pop's didn't. The down pillow appeared fluffed, the covers were pulled up tight enough to bounce a half-dollar on and folded back about six inches at the top.

That feeling was there again, in my gut, in my heart. The voice. Something was wrong.

"Maybe they went outside to go to the bathroom," Henry said, still studying Pop's queerly vacant cot. "You know how his bladder's been shrinking. You can tell time by his peeing schedule.

Every hour on the hour. It don't change at night."

I shook my head. "I don't think so. Look—" I pointed to the far side of the cabin, toward Pop's bed, "—he left his slippers."

"Maybe—"

"And his boots. And I didn't hear anything outside." Pop's boots sat at the foot of his cot, side by side, laces tucked inside. He was either barefooted or stocking-footed, but he was definitely shoeless.

Henry threw the covers back and sat on the edge of his cot. He handed me the light and rubbed his face again. "Okay. Let's get changed and go outside. See what they're up to."

As I hurriedly slipped into a pair of trousers and pulled on my canvas field jacket, a sense of fear crept into my chest, and my heart picked up its tempo. Maybe it was nothing, maybe they were just watering saplings, maybe Pop just needed some fresh air, or got sick, or anything. I tried to be positive, fill my head with logical reasons why two grown men would vacate a semi-warm cabin in the middle of the night, leaving their cots in such odd shape. One looked like its occupant planned to leave, like two o'clock in the morning was a perfectly natural time to exit a cabin and brave the outdoors in near pitch darkness. The other was left in a hurry, like nature had called and wasn't taking no or wait or later for an answer. But no matter how hard I tried to be optimistic, no matter how many scenarios I conjured in my mind, one kept coming back to me, a freight train of doubt looping through my head—someone was in trouble. Cold fingers of fear tickled the back of my neck, and my throat suddenly tightened. I clenched my fists then blotted my hands on my pants. My palms had taken to sweating.

"You ready?" Henry asked, standing beside me, shotgun in hand.

I took a deep breath. "Yeah, I'm ready."

"You man the light, I'll handle the gun."

Whether he meant it or not, which I doubt he did, the command came off as degrading. As if I *couldn't* handle the gun. As if I was only man enough to bear the light. I didn't take it personally. Henry wasn't the antagonistic type—that was Dad. Henry was more brawn than brain, and all heart. At six-two and nearly two hundred and twenty pounds, he was wound tight and thickly muscled. With wide hands and broad shoulders he was proportioned like Dad—built to work. Problem was, Henry was a bit of a lug. Strong, yes. Coordinated, no. His movements were usually slow and determined, concentrated, as if coordinating the various muscles to perform even a simple task was a chore of immense proportion. I, on the other hand, with my long, slender fingers, narrow shoulders and hips, and lithe five-ten frame, took after Mom's side of the family: Grandfather was a doctor, Uncle Mitchell a lawyer. I dreamed of being a preacher or theologian one day. Doctoring people's souls, counseling their spirits.

But I'd be lying if I said there wasn't a part of me that wished I were built like Henry and Dad, that imagined myself with shoulders like stone blocks and hands like baseball mitts, that secretly fantasized about braving the wild outdoors and taking down a black bear with a barrel full of lead.

Henry opened the door to the outside, turned and looked at me. "You okay?"

17

"Yeah." My voice quavered a bit. "I'd be more comfortable with a gun in my hands, though."

Looking at me as though I had asked for a bazooka, Henry shook his head and said, "No, Bill. I need you on the light. If we get into trouble, how will I know what to shoot at if I can't even see it? Besides, when's the last time you fired a gun? I don't want you going and mistaking me for the boogeyman and blowing a hole the size of a cow pie in my back." He nodded at the electric lantern in my hand and when he spoke again his voice had upped a couple of notches on the serious scale. "You man the light. It's as important as pulling the trigger. Maybe more so."

Henry wasn't a philosopher by any definition of the word, he wasn't a contemplator, wasn't a logician, and would probably be on the losing side of a political debate with a monkey. But he was a farmer and farm folk have a unique brand of common horse sense, homespun philosophy, which academic types pass off as being hokey or trite but secretly envy though they could never hope to understand it nor acquire it. The wisdom of farm folk is learned and honed and sharpened through hard work and keeping their noses to the grind when life throws all kinds of manure their way. The value of family and bonding and good living is taught and learned from the time they can carry a pitchfork and muck out a horse stall. Their wisdom is the wisdom of the ages, not gleaned from some heavy-minded, big-headed academic in a stuffy, ivy-encased university, but harvested from experience, from pain, from love, mistakes and victories—the stuff of life fully-lived.

Henry was right, I probably *would* blow a hole the size of a cow pie in his back if I mistook him for the villainous boogeyman.

I hadn't held a gun to my shoulder and squeezed the trigger in close to four years. And *someone* had to hold the light. We certainly couldn't go traipsing around in the wild outdoors in the middle of a moonless morning, blind as deaf bats, with two loaded weapons, one handled by a trigger-happy, weak-bellied, boogeyman-slayer.

"Okay," I said. "Point made and taken."

Steadying my hands against the seismic tremble that had overcome them, pushing saliva down my throat, willing my heart to resume a moderate rate and even rhythm, and manning the light like it could spit flamethrower fire, I followed Henry outside into the untamed darkness.

Antagonists people love to hate

And now a word about antagonists. Villains. Bad guys. These are the folks we love to hate. But be careful here. You don't want to create a cardboard, cookie cutter villain who is all bad and predictable. Remember, we're creating fictional characters but we want the reader to feel like they're real people. And real people are complicated. When creating your antagonist be careful to give him something he wrestles with internally. Maybe a horrid past or some personality disorder or mental health issue. We want to create a bad guy who isn't all bad. We want something there that the reader can empathize with and almost sympathize with. Infants just don't grow up to be evil people. There are reasons this happens. Tap into those reasons. Show the reader the history behind the villain, how he became evil. It's a process with most people, a slow fade that goes deeper and deeper and gets darker and darker. Show that decline into darkness.

Also, most people are duplicitous. Meaning, they have two or more sides to their personality. How many times have you heard neighbors say of serial killers, "But he was such a nice guy. I never would have expected he would do something like this." Allow your antagonist to be duplicitous. This keeps the reader off-balance and adds a level of much-needed suspense whether you're writing a suspense novel or not.

Read below our first introduction to the antagonists in *Fear Mountain.* There are four of them, some more evil than others but all are bad guys you just love to hate. Notice the anxiety and brutality that surrounds these guys as soon as they are introduced to the reader.

My eyelids felt like they were weighted with musket balls. My head throbbed like someone was on the inside trying to get out with a ball peen hammer. With my eyes still closed and my head swimming in murky water, I sensed that I was indoors, lying on my right side on a hard floor. My back ached, and my right hip and leg were numb. I could hear muffled movements to my left, breathing to my right. I tried to move, lift myself off the floor and was quickly scolded by a sharp pain in my shoulders. A guttural groan escaped my dry mouth.

Something nudged me in my shoulder. Then again, harder. Then a string of harshly-spoken German words. I caught the words "open" and "eyes" and thought it best to do as I was told. At least,

I hoped I was being ordered to "Open your eyes" and not "*Don't open your eyes.*" Slowly, I lifted my lids, blinked several times, and let my eyes focus. A large man with a square head sitting atop broad shoulders stood over me. He had a thick crop of light brown hair, dusted with gray, and a full wiry beard that hid most of his wide and weathered face. In his right hand he held a black pistol, pointed at the floor. He looked at me with narrowed eyes and snorted.

"*Dummen Amerikaner. Aufstehen!*" My German was coming back to me. I was being called a stupid American and told to get up. And though my legs were numb and heavy I thought it best to at least attempt to obey my captor.

I tried to sit, tried to pull my torso up off the floor, but with my arms bound behind my back and every movement sending electric jolts through my shoulders, I only grunted and groaned but got nowhere. I was able to lift my head and begin a feeble roll but that was as far as I got.

The German reached down and grabbed a handful of my jacket at the shoulder, yanked me to a sitting position, then shoved me back down so I was lying on my arms behind me. Pain shot across my shoulders and momentarily paralyzed me.

Again, I received a nudge with the boot and an order, "*Aufstehen.*" Stand up. He said it in a calm voice, as if he were telling me to eat my bratwurst.

I tried again, but again my attempts proved futile. My muscles were too dead, shoulders too sore, right side too numb. I wasn't going anywhere.

Again the German nudged me—"*Aufstehen*"—and this

time I caught a hint of irritation in his voice.

"I can't," I said, wondering if he understood any English at all. I didn't want to say "No" for fear that he would interpret it as insolence and feel a need to display his advantage over me. My survival depended on my ability to stay calm and oblige my subjugator as best I could.

He looked at me with those narrow eyes then pressed his lips into a thin line. Reaching down, he took a grip on my jacket again and lifted me to a sitting position. Blood thumped through my head, and my eyesight blurred from the pain. When things came into focus again, I noticed I was in a small room alone with the German. There was no furniture, no carpet, no wall hangings. The two windows were covered with torn shades, allowing only stray beams of sunlight to illuminate the room with muted, dirty light. The hardwood floor was dusty and gray. Long jagged cracks split the ceiling plaster into three even sections.

The German squatted next to me, his face only inches from mine. It was then I noticed how dark his eyes were. I could barely tell where the irises stopped and the pupils started. His forehead was broad and thick and his nose boxy and red. He looked hardened and tough. Not someone I wanted to anger.

He said it again, this time cutting each syllable with a sharp edge. *"Aufstehen."* A speck of spittle landed on his lower lip.

Careful not to shake my head (the universal sign for "No" and defiance) I said in as calm a voice as I could muster. "I don't think I can." Still my voice cracked and quavered.

The big German stood tall, towering over me like Goliath over another victim, and pointed the pistol at my head.

"Aufstehen.. Jetzt."

My heart punched the inside of my chest. If I didn't appear cooperative, I would have no chance of surviving this. And if I didn't survive chances were strong Dad and Pop and Henry wouldn't either. Once this brute got his temperature up and blood on his hands, there would be no telling where he'd stop. I struggled to get my legs under me but with my right side in its present state of deadness and my arms out of service, my attempt proved fruitless. My mind told my legs to move, but my muscles weren't getting the message.

I looked at my captor, searching his granite face for any sign of pity and found none. "I can't," I said again, hoping, praying, he would understand, if not my words then at least my body language.

"Aufstehen!" he hollered, then raised the gun as if to bring it down hard on my head.

I flinched and shut my eyes waiting for the blow that would once again turn off the lights. But it never came. Instead I heard laughter. Not happy laughter, but mocking laughter. I slowly opened my eyes. The German, hands on his hips, glared at me, laughing with a broad, evil grin stretched across his hairy face.

"Dummen Amerikaner." Then in one quick, fluid motion, the smile disappeared, a shadow fell over his eyes, his hand lifted, and he brought the pistol down against my head.

Okay, now to humanize the antagonists. This scene below gives the reader a little insight into the depth of mental darkness that torments the villains.

No more than ten minutes passed before the smaller of the quartet poked his head around the corner and gave me that coyote smile again—wide, flat grin, ears pulled back, eyes narrowed—and nodded at me. He disappeared for a second then entered the room, walking lightly on the floorboards. He sat Indian-style on the floor across from me, clasped both hands in his lap, and leaned forward like a child ready to share a secret. His skin was an odd off-white, almost translucent, which made his eyes look even darker. His beard covered most of his jaw line but was patchy and thin; he couldn't have been any older than Aaron. Somewhere in Germany there may have been a seventeen-year old thinking about his older brother in some forest in America, wondering if they would ever be reunited. But chances were my German counterpart wasn't in the hands of psychotic American bandits.

Coyote licked his lips with a small pink tongue and began to slowly rock back and forth, a look of wonderment brightening his face. Suddenly, he stopped and leaned forward again. "I vas at Auschwitz." He said it in broken English in a low voice laced with excitement, like it was a Christmas secret he could keep no longer from me.

"You speak English," I said.

Coyote looked surprised that I would make such a statement, like I had deeply hurt his feelings. "I vent to University," he said. "to study music." His eyes dropped to his hands, and he studied his long, slender fingers for a few moments. "I apologize my English is not better. Is very difficult language to learn."

"Who are you?" I asked, hoping to get some information

24

out of him, some explanation of how four German Nazis came to be wandering around the woods of Maine and why they would take four Americans captive.

"At Auschwitz, ze first thing you see when you enter the compound are the vords *Arbeit Macht Frei.*" He looked at me with wide eyes. "Do you know vhat they mean, ze vords?"

I absently answered, "Work makes one free."

"*Ja.* They think vork makes one free, but they are wrong. It is lie. Only death frees." He looked around the room, then found something interesting about one of his fingernails, picking at it with the thumbnail of his other hand.

"Why are you here?" I tried again to pry some information from my new friend.

Instead of answering my inquiry, Coyote clasped his hands again and smiled at me. "Oh, ze people ve set free. Millions. An ocean of souls, trapped in dying bodies, that ve . . . I . . . had great privilege of setting free. Releasing from prison of flesh."

My stomach tightened and the taste of bile burned the back of my throat. Auschwitz was the largest and most infamous of the Nazi death camps. Some reports were surfacing that said as many as four million Poles, Soviets, Gypsies, and Jews were murdered there. Most by gas, some by starvation, torture, shooting, and medical "experiments." The atrocities committed there by the Nazis were on a hellish scale, and the world had been reeling from the gruesome reality since the Soviets liberated the camp in January.

With a faraway look in his dark eyes, Coyote licked his lips again and said, "Auschwitz is great place, a gift from God. A place

25

vere freedom rings. Is that not vhat you Americans say about your homeland? Freedom rings from mountaintops? But true freedom, *real* freedom is found at Auschwitz."

"The war is over," I said, "and you lost. Auschwitz was liberated by the Soviets. It's over." I enjoyed the way the words sounded to my own ears. *You lost. It's over.* There was something sweet and vengeful about them.

"Lost? No my friend, ve cannot lose. Our struggle is not vith flesh and blood, you see. Ve battle principalities and powers, spiritual foes that battle for souls. It is never over."

Either Coyote had been brainwashed into believing this nonsense he was uttering or he was grandly deluded. Either way, a man who saw death as freedom and murdering innocents as liberation was not the friend I wanted to make in my present circumstance. In the spirit of friendship, he was apt to feel compassion on me and set me free. And his freedom was not the freedom I sought. Given the choice, I'd have taken my chances with a real coyote.

Coyote ran his pink tongue over his lips again and continued. "I vas stationed at gas chamber." His eyes fell on mine, and I felt the weight of the evil that lurked inside him, like a hungry crocodile prowling a swamp just below the water's surface. I didn't want to hear anymore. "You should have seen look on their faces vhen they realized they vere not taking showers, merely cleaning dirt from their bodies, but having their souls vashed and freed. Oh, ze joy, ze bliss that covered them. They even danced with delight. A beautiful, poetic dance, hundreds of them, singing, dancing."

Forget the brainwashing, my dog-faced friend was delusional. The gas chambers were equipped with showerheads that released cyanide. Cyanide causes seizures right before death. What he interpreted as dancing and singing was something much more grisly.

Coyote unfolded himself and stood. He bowed slightly and donned an eager grin. "Ve vill talk again soon."

I watched as he exited the room, hands behind his back, head bowed as if in reverent thought. He descended the stairs with light footfalls.

And then I was alone in the room, alone with my fears and questions. Were Dad and Pop and Henry in the house? Were they still alive? Or had Coyote "freed" them already? Was I next to experience his demented form of liberty? Cold chills traced tracks across my skin, raising goosebumps along the length of my arms. I tried to pray but words didn't seem adequate; it would have to do to just allow my spirit to groan.

One more word about antagonists. Your "villain" doesn't have to be a human at all. Sometimes the monsters that hunt us are not flesh and blood. Sometimes it's cancer or a tornado or a disability or a savage past that haunts us. Don't feel like the antagonist who torments your main character has to be a person.

"Wise old sage"

This is not a necessary character but can be a very useful character. And, yes, it does mimic real life. The "wise old sage" character is seen in literature of all kinds and forms and has been for centuries. This is the character who keeps the protagonist on the right path, who offers advice or admonition when needed. This is the character who feeds the protagonist appropriate information at the right time and thereby feeds the reader needful information to keep the story going. This is not a major character but rather a secondary one. He or she shows up when needed to offer guidance, advice, wisdom or to give insight into what is going on. Sometimes he or she encourages the protagonist or scolds him, sometimes he challenges the protagonist to do the right thing or gives evidence of what the right thing to do is.

In short, most of us have one of these "sages" in our life. A parent, a grandparent, a teacher, a co-worker, a mentor of some kind. Someone who is there when we need him or her and gives the kind of advice we need to hear at the time. Someone who challenges us or encourages us or shakes a finger in our face when needed.

In this scene from *Fear Mountain*, Peter, a man who befriends our protagonist offers some much-needed guidance.

> Peter lifted his eyes away from the fire and looked at me. Shadows and light from the flame played tricks with the angles of his face, making him look much older. "For what?"
>
> I tipped my head in the direction of the woods behind Peter. "The bear. I was so scared I almost wet my pants. I thought I was a goner."
>
> Without smiling, Peter said, "You were. She was in a really bad mood and I think you gave her a good scare."

I didn't know what to say to that so I just nodded and went back to my trance.

After a long moment of silence had passed between Peter and me, I broke a stick in two and tossed half of it into the fire, then said, "Will we catch up to them tomorrow?"

Peter poked at the hot red embers beneath the fire with a long, twisted stick. "Yes." His voice was tight, like he was being strangled, or strangling himself.

He stopped poking and the sudden abruptness of the act coupled with the tight quality of his voice caused me to pull my eyes away from the flames and fix them on his face. There were tears in his eyes.

"What's the matter? What's going on?" I knew enough by now to know that Peter was not just the teary-eyed, blubbery type. When his eyes leaked, it was for a reason: something ominous was about to happen. I felt a weight as heavy as an anvil descend from the morose sky and settle on my chest. The air seemed to thicken to the consistency of mom's rice pudding. And I was certain the flames grew angrier, snapping with more ferocity than before. "What is it, Peter?"

Peter sat quietly for a minute or so, eyes staring blankly at the fire as if he would find an answer, *the* answer to the oppressive problem that had found us. When no answer materialized, he looked up at me and our eyes met. There was no sadness in his gaze, but fear. Not scream-in-the-night, boogeyman-under-your-bed fear, nor was it kissed-by-your-300-pound-mustached-Aunt-Louise fear, but it was a subtle fear that came from the deepest, darkest, catacombs of the unknown where nightmares are birthed and phobias find their fangs.

His Adam's apple jerked in his throat, and he wiped a tear from the corner of his mouth. "Tomorrow . . . Billy, are you capable of trusting? I mean, *really* trusting?" He said it like it was the last thing he would say on this earth and his and my eternal future depended on my ability to trust.

"Yes," I said before even thinking about my answer.

Peter studied me as one would study a Van Gogh masterpiece, picking up every brush stroke, every tint of color, every subtlety in shading and shadowing. Finally, he said, "Trust, Billy. You have to trust."

I didn't know what he was getting at. I consider myself a fairly intelligent person. I love to read all sorts of books and fill my head with knowledge for which I'll probably never have any practical use, but one thing I lack is discernment, especially when it pertains to the emotions and affections of others. I know my family members well enough, but when it comes to strangers I'm as lost and blind as a moose in the Mojave. "I trust you," I said to Peter with a hint of annoyance in my voice.

"Not just *me*," he snapped, showing as close to anger as he'd shown thus far. Something had him wound tight. Something serious. "Oh please don't place all your trust in me alone."

"I don't know what you're getting at, Peter? If not you, then who?"

"*Him*," he said and by the way he said it I knew who he was talking about. God. Peter was asking me if I could trust, really trust, God. "Can you place your hopes and dreams, your convictions and passions, your sense of reality, in *His* hands?"

"I think I can." It was the best I could do. I'd always thought I could place all my trust in God alone, I believed in Him and had given my life to Him. I believed He was sovereign and good and holy and always had my best interest in mind, but I'd never really had my mettle, my faith, tested to the fullest. Not like it was being tested now. "Yes, I can."

Peter didn't look satisfied at my answer. He turned his eyes toward the flame, studied their gyrations for a few seconds until a fresh stream of tears slipped down his cheek, then looked at me again. "You'll have to trust tomorrow. Trust me, yes, but most of all trust God, Billy. No matter what happens, trust God. For your sake and for the sake of your dad and brother and grandfather."

I knew he was getting at something, knew something I didn't, and in his cryptic, mysterious way was warning me about whatever it was. I also knew I didn't like being in the dark, either literally or figuratively. "What are you getting at? What's going to happen tomorrow?"

More tears poured from Peter's eyes, and he let them flow uninhibited. The man I saw sitting across the fire from me, his face aglow from the flames, rivulets of tears glistening like wet glass, was not the same man who rescued me from the cellar and sure death, nor was he the same man who led me through the woods to the safety of a secret hiding place. This wasn't even the same man who'd just faced down Mama Bear and declined a spot on her dance card. He was a tortured soul, wrestling with knowledge he wished he didn't possess, grappling with a future that looked as dark as the sky above us.

His red-rimmed, puffy eyes met mine; his chin quivered. "Billy, no matter what happens tomorrow, trust. Trust God. He will show you." He then unfolded his legs and stood, looking down at the fire as if to say goodbye to a long-lost friend after a brief but very emotional reunion. "He will see you through."

Secondary characters

Though they aren't the main attraction these characters are very important to the story as a whole and the life of the protagonist and/or antagonist. Secondary characters serve to fill out the life of the main characters. They are the people the main characters talk to, interact with, they provide dialogue and conflict. We should care about these characters. Not as much as we care about the protagonist but enough that what they say and do matters.

Think of your list of characters as a cast in a movie. The protagonist is one of the main characters, of which there may only be a few. The secondary characters are the folks the main characters interact with. They receive a good amount of screen time but not as much as the main characters. We know something about their lives, where they come from, what they do, and how they feel, but again, not as much as the main characters.

The main thing to keep in mind when creating secondary characters is that (1) their existence must be purposeful, and (2) we must care about them.

They must serve a specific purpose. They can't show up just to hold mundane conversations with the main characters or do insignificant things. They may do that but it can't be the only thing they do. They must have a purpose. Their existence must mean something.

And we have to care about them. We have to care about what they say, how they say it, what kind of loyalty they show the main character, what kind of trouble they get into. If they don't matter to the story or the main characters they won't matter to the reader.

Fear Mountain doesn't have a lot of secondary characters but two primary ones are Billy's dad and brother, Henry. In this scene notice how the reader is tuned into Billy's relationship with his brother which will be of some importance later on in the story.

Henry slowed so I could come alongside him. Massaging the stock of the gun with both hands, he cleared his throat, glanced my way, then said, "Is it my fault Dad got . . . taken?"

I knew he thought it was his fault, I could detect the pain in his tight voice, but he wanted me to assure him it wasn't. "First," I said, "we don't know if Dad was taken, or Pop, we just know they're missing is all. And if he was taken, how could it be your fault?"

He started to say something then paused. He'd stopped massaging the gun, but his eyes darted back and forth along the trail. "You wanted to take him back to the cabin and when he fussed I didn't support you. I let him have his way and stay out there by himself because I was afraid of disappointing him. Afraid of *him.* You were right. We should have taken him back even if we had to hogtie him and drag him by his feet."

"But even if we had taken him back, whoever did that to the cabin would have found him there just as easily as they found him by the tree. I don't see the logic there. And we could have been in the cabin when they came . . . who knows what would have happened. We might all be dead right now, on that cabin floor, all full of lead."

Henry stopped and stared at nothing in particular to his right.

"What—"

He held up a hand, silencing me mid-sentence. He'd heard something. I noticed his chest had stopped rising and falling. After a few seconds he lowered his hand, looked at me, then glanced one more time back into the woods. "I thought I heard something."

He started walking again and I followed.

"If he was in the cabin," Henry continued, "he could have defended himself with the guns. Could have put up a fight at least. And if we were there, *we* could have put up a fight, protected what's ours. They took him from right under our noses, Billy. We didn't even hear anything."

I hadn't thought of that before. I took my mind back several hours. We were combing the area where we'd last heard Pop's groans, kicking leaves around as we walked, making a lot of noise. Possibly too much to hear someone restraining Dad and carrying him off. Dad was a big man, though, and it would take more than one person to subdue him unless they knocked him out cold first . . . or killed him. That last thought sickened me. My imagination immediately conjured an image of some devil sneaking up behind

34

Dad and slitting his throat, then throwing him over its shoulder and carrying him away as he left a trail for us to follow . . . possibly to meet the same fate.

While we were kicking up leaves, looking for anything that would clue us into Pop's whereabouts, I'd found the pillbox. *Gott mit uns.* We'd immediately abandoned the search to return to Dad and show him the box. We ran to him, again making enough noise to deafen us to a struggle that may have been taking place only yards away.

It was stupid of us to make so much noise. We should have known better. *I* should have known better. I didn't dare share my sentiments with Henry, though. He'd already beaten himself up with guilt and was toting a heavy enough burden. I didn't need to pile more blame on him.

"We were making a lot of noise," I finally said. "We had no idea he was in danger. How could we have known?"

Henry kept walking and didn't say anything.

About a half hour later he stopped and pushed around some leaves with his boot. "It's gone. The trail."

I bent over, rested my hands on my knees, and studied the ground. Sure enough, no leaves were disturbed, no marks of any kind on the exposed soil.

Henry looked behind us, back down the mountain, scanning the path we'd just forged through thick underbrush and over rocky ground. "I don't know how long ago we lost it," he said, his voice thick with despair and near-panic.

"What do you mean?"

"I mean I've been thinking about things, trying to figure all this out, and just walking. I don't know how long we've been walking and I haven't been following any trail. Just walking."

Again, I knew he blamed himself. He was really giving himself a whipping.

I approached him, stood by his side, and put a hand on his shoulder. "It's okay, Henry. Really. I wasn't paying attention either. Let's just backtrack until we pick it up again. There's still plenty of daylight. If we go back down the same way we came up we should run into the trail, right?"

By then the sun was nearing its full height in the sky and was almost directly overhead. Its rays filtered through the canopy of leaves and dappled the ground with a mosaic of spotted light. Birds chirped cheerily in the trees above us, to our right a squirrel chattered angrily, warning us away from its secret nut stash. If not for the dire circumstances that necessitated our hike, and if not for my fear of being left alone in the woods again, it would have been an enjoyable afternoon spent in the woods.

Henry agreed and we returned back down the mountain the way we had come. After some time, we both realized we'd lost our way again. With no clear trail marking our progress and the tangle of brush and shrubs that covered the ground it was easy to meander off course and lose our bearings.

After roaming around for nearly the whole afternoon, looking for anything that would point us in the right direction—a blood droplet, a scuff mark, a road sign—and after watching the look of frustration and hopelessness deepen on Henry's face, I started to feel like our rescue mission was a miserable failure. I reasoned that when we didn't return home the day after tomorrow as planned, Mom would worry and tell Uncle Will (who was manning the farm while we were gone) to go to the cabin and retrieve us. He would find the cabin empty and pillaged, go for help, and a search party would be assembled. If we could survive that long, help would be on the way. *If* we could survive that long. Watching Henry slide deeper and deeper into a miry pit of anguish, I wasn't sure he'd last another night. His guilt and self-loathing would rapidly grow weightier. It was only a matter of time before, out of sheer desperation, he did something reckless and endangered both of us.

I was about to offer some words of encouragement in hopes of allaying the impending storm when Henry suddenly stopped and stooped low, holding a hand behind him to stop me. He looked back, held one finger to his mouth, then pointed up ahead. I followed his finger and peered through the columns of oaks and maples. There, in the distance, about fifty yards ahead, was a small clearing, and off to the left of the clearing stood a house.

Other characters

Okay, these are the characters who are basically in the story to populate the fictional world you've created. We interact with these people every day in the real world. They are the store clerks, shoppers, travelers, pedestrians, tourists . . . people all around us every day. Some we talk to, some we avoid, some we wholly ignore, some we just watch with a certain curiosity. To make your fictional world come alive your story must include these people. They become part of the description, props. Your main and secondary characters may have interactions with them or they may not. Sometimes they will reveal information for the reader but it's not necessary.

Additional Reading:

Writer's Digest: "How to Craft Compelling Characters"

http://www.writersdigest.com/writing-articles/by-writing-goal/write-first-chapter-get-started/hooked-on-a-feeling

Novel Writing Help: "The First Rule of Creating Fictional Characters"

http://www.novel-writing-help.com/creating-fictional-characters.html

Your turn:

Assignment 1: Create a biographical sketch of an original protagonist of your choosing. Describe his or her appearance, background, character traits. Talk about his or her strengths and weaknesses. What motivates him or her? What does he or she fear? What kind of family life does he or she have? (at least 400 words)

Assignment 2: Create a biographical sketch of an original antagonist of your choosing. Describe his or her appearance, background, character traits. Talk about his or her strengths and weaknesses. What motivates him or her? What does he or she fear? What kind of family life does he or she have? (at least 400 words)

Section 2

PLOT

The plot is the story itself. It's what's happening. You have a main character and she has to do something. Then you have stuff working against her to keep her from doing it. From finding love to finding a lost child. That's plot. It's the story.

The basic element of any good story is conflict. There has to be conflict, tension involved. Becky needs to find love but there's a whole bunch of stuff working against her. Plot. Conflict. Jeff needs to rescue his daughter but there are many obstacles in his way, including the villain. Plot. Conflict. See it?

Conflict rules. And the more conflict, the more obstacles and hurdles and mud the protagonist has to sludge through, the better the plot, the more intriguing the story.

Nobody wants to read a story about a man mowing his lawn. It's boring, it's mundane, it's too everyday normal. But what if he's trying to mow his lawn but the mower keeps shutting off on him? We add a little bit of conflict. And what if it keeps shutting off on him because his neighbor sabotaged it? Okay, more conflict. And what if his neighbor sabotaged it because he's jealous of Jeff's perfect lawn. Okay, now we have way more conflict. See the story developing? Conflict. The more the better.

The same goes for stakes. The higher the stakes for the protagonist the better. Let's take our example with Jeff. So his neighbor hates his perfect lawn and is jealous. Okay, that's bad but what would make it worse? What would really raise the stakes high for Jeff? How about that his neighbor is absolutely crazy and wants to completely become Jeff and assume his role as husband of Jeff's wife and father to Jeff's children . . . and owner of Jeff's perfect lawn. He wants Jeff out of the picture and will do whatever it takes to get the job done. Now the stakes are pretty high. Life or death. And Jeff's family is in the crosshairs. That's pretty high stakes. As authors we want to raise the stakes so high that the reader is literally on the edge of her seat from the intensity. And this goes for romance or historicals or contemporary fiction too. Raise those stakes. Make it really important stuff. You know, there are things in life that seem like they matter and then there are things that really matter. High stakes put the things that really matter on the edge and threaten to push them off.

Plot elements

Back story . . .

Back story is used to give the reader more information about a character, to reveal motivation or history. It places the character in history. We all exist in the here and now but we all have histories, baggage we carry. Things have happened in our past that have played a role in molding us into the people we are today.

Your main characters should be no different. They should be fully-formed three-dimensional people with a context in history.

Back story should not be dumped on the reader. Avoid long, drawn out sections of back story. The goal of storytelling is to move a story forward and by its very nature back story takes it backward. But overall, any back story that is shared must be necessary to the story as a whole and it must reveal traits about a character or motivations. Also, back story should be used conservatively. Sprinkle back story scenes into the story like a strong spice, a little here, a little there.

Entire scenes. You can set an entire scene aside to devote to something that happened to the character in the past. This will read like any other scene in the book except it takes place at some point in the past. You'll want to give the reader some clue as to the time period of the scene. Is it last week or twenty years ago?

Flashbacks. These can be full scenes or snippets of thoughts, memories, visions, or dreams. These are used more to focus on a specific event.

Dialogue. Two or more characters discuss events that took place in the past.

Narrative. The narrator (speaking as the point-of-view character) mentions events that took place in the past, thus allowing the reader to gain knowledge about the character's history otherwise impossible to know.

Story Arc . . .

Every story must follow an arc. The arc goes something like this: introduction—rising action—climax—resolution. You'll find other descriptions in other writings but this is the basic arc.

Introduction. This is usually the first two or three chapters and it introduces the characters and problem/conflict to the reader. Lots of questions should be formed here, lots of mystery, intrigue. This is the time to set the stage for the story. No answers are given and character back stories should only be touched on.

Rising action. This is the bulk of the story. As the story progresses the conflict should build. Obstacles for the protagonist should multiply. The suspense should intensify. By the end of the rising action it should appear that there is no way the story can be resolved, that our protagonist is simply in a no-win situation.

Climax. This is where it all comes to a head. Where forces clash and the conflict just explodes. This is the part everyone looks forward to. It's where the protagonist and antagonist finally go head to head.

Resolution. This is usually the last chapter or two and it wraps up loose ends, answers remaining questions, and provides some closure to the story. Now, a word about the resolution. You don't have to answer all the questions and not all the loose ends need to be wrapped up, only the most important ones. We don't always get answers to all our questions in real life and we don't get all those loose ends wrapped up nice and tidy. And since we want our fiction to reflect real life we need to leave some sense of reality at the end of the story. But note, the most important questions and issues need to be resolved in a believable way or your reader will feel cheated.

Think about popular stories you know or ones you've read and examine how this introduction—rising action—climax—resolution arc takes place.

For instance, let's look at Cinderella, a story most everyone is familiar with. The **introduction** is the opening scenes where we are literally introduced to the characters and told a little of Cinderella's story. We meet Cinderella, the step-mother and the two awful step-sisters. We learn that Cinderella's father died and she was left alone with her step-family. The **rising action** is the bulk of the story. Things are bad for Cinderella but they only get worse. She wants to go to the ball but her step-mother and sisters are determined to thwart her dream. Finally, she does get to go (notice her fairy godmother is the "wise old sage" character) but even that ends in conflict. At the end of the rising action section we think things can't get any worse for poor Cinderella. She'll never get out of that house. Then the **climax** comes. This is when we find out the slipper does indeed fit Cinderella and there is the confrontation with the step-mother and sisters. Finally, the **resolution**. We learn that Cinderella marries the prince and all is well. We also learn an important lesson about Cinderella's character as well. She is quite the forgiving person.

Do you see it? Most stories follow this arc and you can take almost any story and plug the overall plot into these four basic sections. Try it with some of your favorites.

Additional Reading:

Screencraft: "5 Ways to Create Conflict in Your Story"

https://screencraft.org/2014/05/13/ways-create-conflict-story-script-screenplay/

Writer's Relief: "Stop Sagging Middle Syndrome: 5 Plot Devices That Will Amp Up Your Story" http://writersrelief.com/blog/2013/07/sagging-middle-syndrome-plot-devices/

Your turn:

Create a basic outline for a short story, highlighting the introduction, rising action, climax, and resolution. Write on paragraph for each element of the story arc. (at least 400 words)

Section 3

DESCRIPTION

Description allows the reader to see what you've written, to see the characters, the world in which they live, the action. If done right, good description will allow the reader to see the story playing out in his mind like a movie. So how much description is enough and how much is too much? That's an important question for the writer to ponder with every scene. And it will vary depending on the mood you want to convey in the scene.

A few things to keep in mind . . .

There's a balance that must be found between not enough description and too much description. Not enough description will leave the reader feeling short-changed. She will be reading words but not be able to see the scene playing out in real time. It will just be words on a page, flat, meaningless. Too much description will bore the reader. It's just too many needless details that slow the pace to a grinding halt and make you, the author, come off as a wordy windbag. And you never want the reader to see you as a windbag.

When thinking about description and how much to use we must take into account the average reader in the 21st Century. We live in a "right now" culture.

Things happen fast. We have fast food and instant messaging. Our attention span has been reduced to mere minutes. Readers get bored with too much description and "too much" is less now than it was even a few decades ago. Keep that in mind. When describing a setting or action sequence I always try to give enough description so the reader can see what's going on but not too much to take away from the scene and bore him. You want your description to always add to the scene not detract from it. Also, how much description you include will depend on the pace of the scene. Fast-paced scenes will naturally have less description of setting and more of action and slow-paced scenes will have more description of setting, most likely not so much of action.

Try to work at least three of the five senses into every scene. Sometimes this isn't possible but try when it is possible. Show the reader what the setting, characters, and action looks like. Show them what it smells like, what it feels like to the characters, and what the characters hear and taste. Here are some suggestions:

What does the point-of-view (POV) character see? Other characters, buildings, trees, the sky, the terrain, birds in the air. Give the reader a full 360 view of the setting the character is in.

What does the POV character hear? People talking, cars, wind in the trees, birds, lawn mowers. A good way to get better at this is to close your eyes in various settings and just listen. What do you hear? What sounds can you pick up on that you hadn't noticed before?

What does the POV character feel? The wind on his skin, another character's touch, pain, sweaty clothes sticking to her skin, the feel of salt water in her hair. Let the reader feel what the character feels.

What does the POV character smell? Smoke, burning rubber, burning flesh, the aroma of flowers, fresh cut grass. Again, let the reader smell what the character smells. And again, a good way to improve at this is to pay particular attention to the smells you encounter in different settings.

What does the POV character taste? Various kinds of food, the metallic taste of blood, bile, smoke. Pay attention to the various tastes you experience in a day and think about how you would describe them.

Description is so important to creating a full world for your characters to inhabit and to pull the reader into that world.

Now, another note on description. Use similes and metaphors so the reader can relate to your descriptions. Similes use "like" or "as" and draw a comparison between two things. For instance, He set his jaw like stone. Metaphors are used in a more symbolic way and apply a word or phrase directly to an object or action. For instance, His jaw was stone. The character's jaw wasn't actually stone but the image of stone is symbolic for how he positioned his jaw.

One final thought on description. To improve in your ability to write descriptive prose practice the lost art of observing your surroundings. Watch people. Watch what they do, how they walk, how they dress and stand and interact with one another. Pay attention to non-verbal communication. Body language. Posturing. Take note of the architecture of buildings around you, how sidewalks are positioned, the condition of roads. Listen to the sounds that surround you, pay attention to the textures you encounter, how various fabrics feel against your skin. Take note of how your body feels and reacts in different situations. How does your stomach react, your muscles, your joints? What are you thinking? Feeling? Be aware. Pay attention. It will pay huge dividends when it comes time to create a world for your characters to populate and then describe that world to your readers.

In the following scene from *Fear Mountain*, notice how description is handled. Look for similes and metaphors. Look for the senses being described.

I awoke, startled by an illuminated face just inches from my own. Blankly, my mind a vacuum, I stared at the angelic visage. It wasn't a face I recognized, not Dad or Pop or Henry or any of my new German friends. Not Coyote. At first, I thought I was dreaming, that I'd successfully found freedom and escaped to a far better place than what I'd left behind, a place where people were actually kind and caring and generous, where angels trod and lions reclined with lambs. But when I tried to move and was immediately scolded by an angry throb in my head and a bone-aching gnaw in my shoulders, I knew that place was far from within my reach. But the face, the face of a man, was still there, gleaming. Clean shaven with soft lines and full lips and cerulean eyes that seemed to glow, there was an intensity in the set of his jaw and tightness of his brow that reminded me of the magnitude of my situation.

As the fog cleared from my mind and my surroundings focused I noticed the light that illuminated the man in front of me. It wasn't a yellowish light that might be cast by a candle or bulb, it was white like the light of day at high noon. And it didn't seem to come from any single source but rather spilled over him like soft water. On closer inspection, I also noticed he wasn't holding any light and no light source was nearby. As odd as it felt, it seemed the light was coming from him, as if his skin radiated it, oozed it like sweat or oil.

Darkness still encroached upon us from every corner of the cellar but my visitor and everything a foot out from him glowed like the moon reflecting the brilliant white light of the sun. I marveled at this, at the iridescent quality about the stranger's face, as one would (and should) upon meeting an alien with skin that glowed like the moon's surface, sans craters (his complexion was perfect, as smooth and creamy as buttermilk).

I opened my mouth to question him about who he was, how he got into the cellar, and where the light was coming from when he beat me to it. "Come, we must go now. Quickly."

When he spoke, three things registered in my less-foggy mind and seemed entirely out of place. One, I noticed he looked stereotypically German: short, flax-blonde hair parted neatly to the left and those bluer than blue eyes. Two, he was clothed in the same gray uniform with black belt and boots that my captors wore. And three, he spoke English, with only a hint of a German accent.

He motioned with his hand for me to follow. "Come. Quickly."

I was about to tell him I couldn't because I was tethered to the table leg when my hands slipped free from behind me and fell to my sides. Shoulders feeling like they were filled with cement, I brought my hands slowly in front of me and examined my ropeless wrists. A band of reddened skin encircled them where the rope had dug in.

"Come." His voice was urgent and he bit the word off like you would snap a crisp carrot between your teeth.

I climbed to my feet, my shoulders, back, hips, buttocks, and knees protesting every movement. The stranger led the way through the cellar, and I followed close behind, basking in his glow as if it were a patch of warm sunlight on an overcast chilly day. He led me to the cellar door that opened to the outside world, the same door that Henry had led me to.

"My family," I whispered, reaching for the stranger's shoulder then deciding against it. I didn't know what would happen if I touched him and my hand contacted the odd glow, and now wasn't the time to find out. I pulled my hand back. "I can't leave without my family."

He turned to me and his blue eyes looked like a cloudless sky on a crisp autumn day. I almost expected to see geese pass through them or a single cottony cloud drift by. He held my gaze for a second, just a second, but it was enough to pucker my skin with goosebumps. There was something about those eyes, something . . . powerful, compelling, and if I'd thought of it then I would have said supernatural.

"The time is not right." He said it in an almost musical way, half-singing the words. "All things must happen in their own time, in his time."

It made no sense to me, this stranger's cryptic talk, and I found myself getting irritated. I leaned a little closer and instinctively placed my hand on his upper arm. A warm vibration raced through my hand, traveled up my arm, and settled in my chest. The feeling was similar (I say *similar* because I'd never felt anything like it prior to that moment and haven't since) to laying your hand on the hood of an idling car and letting the vibration cascade through your body.

Immediately, I pulled away. He looked at my hand, then met my eyes again. There was no emotion in his look, only that sense of compulsion.

Feeling the remaining hum of the vibration in my chest, I whispered, "When they find me gone, they'll kill my family. I can't leave them here."

The stranger reached out to touch me, and I pulled my shoulder away, not wanting to experience the peculiar vibration again. He paused, his hand hovering inches from my arm, met my eyes with that powerful stare and nodded ever so subtly. For some reason beyond my comprehension, beyond my ability to adequately explain with words, and despite the uniquely German features and dress, I found myself trusting this strange rescuer. Slowly, he placed his hand on my shoulder. At first I felt nothing, no warmth, no vibration, no buzz or hum or pulsation. But seconds later I felt warmth under his hand, as if it were made of cast iron and he'd just drawn it from a hot stove. The warmth radiated from below his palm and spread throughout my body like hot water, spilling across my shoulders, down my back, down my chest, covering my abdomen then legs.

"In due time," he said, his voice like perfectly sounded notes from an orchestra. "In *his* time." He paused and ministered to me through his eyes, calmed my spirit. "Now come."

He ascended the concrete steps, lifted the door to the outside and exited the cellar first. I followed, close on his heels. The outside world was dark, the twisted branches of the trees painted black against the deep charcoal sky. The area was quiet too. No rodents foraged, no owls hooted.

My rescuer tapped me on the shoulder and motioned for me to follow him. In a crouch, hunched at the waist, I scurried behind him, following his glow as if it were a lighthouse and I a ship lost in the fog. When we passed the tree line, the stranger's radiance dimmed and eventually snuffed out altogether. It reminded me of a candle's flame when the wick burns all the way down and the flame slowly dies. All that's left is an orange glow and a trail of smoke curling into the air. When his glow expired, though, it left behind no orange ember, no afterglow, and no trail of smoke.

Darkness crept in around us like a gaggle of demons, and I lost sight of the stranger. I stood in silence, listening for his footsteps, for the crunch of dry leaves beneath his booted feet, but heard nothing.

"Hey, where are you?" I asked.

There was no answer. I reached out with my hands and felt the dark air. The last time I saw him, right before his light extinguished, he was only two feet from me. Now I felt nothing, only empty space.

"Where are you?" I said again, still whispering so as not to awaken my German hosts and call undue attention to myself.

When no answer came a second time, a sliver of ice slipped down my back.

My rescuer was gone, and I was alone.

Additional Reading:

Denise Robbins: "Description in Fiction"

http://www.deniserobbins.com/articles_description_in_fiction.html

Writing-World.com: "The Art of Description: Eight Tips to Help You Bring Your Settings to Life" http://www.writing-world.com/fiction/description.shtml

The Editor's Blog: "Making Comparisons—Simile and Metaphor in Fiction"

http://theeditorsblog.net/2012/06/06/making-comparisons-simile-and-metaphor-in-fiction/

Your Turn:

Write a scene highlighting the description of setting and action. Dialogue is optional. Use similes and metaphors as appropriate. Include some action in the scene. Be creative. Take the reader there and show us the scene as it plays out. (at least 500 words)

Section 4

POV AND TENSE

Simply put, point-of-view (POV) is which character's eyes the story is being told and seen through. Let's start with the basics, there are three POVs you can write your story from.

First person. This is the character telling the story him/herself. It makes much use of the pronouns "I" and "me". For instance . . . I awoke to the sound of rain tapping on the metal roof above me.

Through the first person POV the story is told as if you were sitting in a room with the protagonist and he is telling you an incredible story of what happened to him. Oftentimes the entire story will be told through this one character's POV.

Second person. Honestly, this is rarely used in fiction but when it is it must be necessary and used effectively. Here, the story is told as if the reader is the POV character. For instance . . . You awaken to the sound of rain tapping on the metal roof above you.

Third person. This is the most-used POV. It makes much use of proper nouns (the names of the characters) and third person pronouns like "he," "she," "them," and "they." For instance . . . Mack awoke to the sound of rain tapping on the metal roof above him.

This is told as if a narrator is telling the story of what happened to each character. Most of the time, stories told in third person will be told from multiple POVs. The protagonist will get the majority of POV scenes, but the antagonist and secondary characters will also get POV scenes.

For our purposes here we will focus solely on first person and third person. Second person is used very infrequently and takes some skill to master; it's more appropriate for an advanced class on fiction writing.

Pros and cons of first person POV. First person allows the reader to intimately be inside the head of the protagonist. She feels everything the character feels, knows her thoughts, motivations, fears, anxieties. It's as if the reader is reliving the story through the protagonist.

The difficult thing with first person is that the reader must spend the entire story stuck inside one person's head. So, if you're going to write a story in first person, make sure the protagonist is a very interesting, unique, gripping character. He or she has to keep the reader intrigued throughout the entire story.

Pros and cons of third person POV. The nice thing about third person is that you can tell the story from multiple POVs so the reader can experience it from a variety of angles. This prevents "character fatigue," the reader getting bored or tired of being inside one character's head the entire story, and it also allows the author to deliver more information to the reader. For instance, in first person the reader will never be inside the villain's head, she will never experience the darkness and agony of his demented psyche. Third person allows this. The reader can be privy to the antagonist's plans and motives which in many cases ramps up the suspense and intrigue.

The difficult thing with third person is writing it in such a way that the reader feels connected to the characters. This is why many writing instructors encourage what is called "deep third person POV." This means you, the narrator, are inside the character's head, showing the reader what the character is thinking, feeling, and planning. Like first person, it allows the reader to have an intimate connection with the character. This confuses many new writers. The best way to explain how to pull this deep POV off is to pretend you're writing the story in first person only you're using third person to describe everything. It's as if the narrator has climbed inside the character and is telling the story from the character's POV.

Here's an example from the first chapter of my book *Kill Devil*. Notice how third person is used to allow the reader to get inside Jed Patrick's head and see what he sees and feel what he feels.

> The weather was about to turn, and a heaviness laced the air, as if the weight of the atmosphere were about to tamp down the forest as the impending tempest crept closer.
>
> Jed Patrick climbed out of his Chevy pick-up and paused a moment to study the western sky. A wall of dark gray clouds, the

leading edge of a massive front, rolled over the bald summit of Rathdrum Mountain like an army of ancient Vikings, having just overtaken the Selkirk range. The air was thick with the smell of ozone and pine as it pushed ahead of the front and through the forest that cloaked the foothills.

Jed shut the truck's door and unscrewed the gas cap. He inserted the nozzle and held it in place, one hand in his pocket. The tank held twenty-six gallons and it guzzled almost every bit of that. He replaced the nozzle on the pump and, rubbing his beard with one hand while screwing the cap in place with the other, glanced once again at the sky. He hadn't seen clouds like that since moving to the Coeur D'Alene area three weeks ago. It was going to be quite the storm.

Making his way across the parking lot, he kept his head down and his baseball cap low. He'd made it three weeks without bringing any attention to himself and he'd like to keep it that way. Folks here were friendly and could get chatty. They wanted to know where you were from, where you were from *originally*, where your family was from, what you were doing in Idaho, what you were doing in Coeur D'Alene, how long you planned to stay, and where you were going to go next. Not that they were skeptical about anyone's arrival in their lovely region of the globe and not that they wanted to dissuade anyone from putting down roots in the Coeur D'Alene area; they were just friendly and talkative and genuinely interested in who was setting up home in their corner of the country. Jed had to be careful to entertain their conversations without giving away too much information but without appearing overly reserved. Either could raise suspicion and draw attention, and that would not work in his favor. Nor in the favor of Karen or Lilly.

Jed had gone to Coeur D'Alene only once since arriving in the area. Their first day in the Coeur D'Alane forest he needed to make a trip to the local superstore to stock the cabin with food and toiletries and other necessities. His plan was then to emerge from the cabin once a week, head to the Mobil on highway 95 and gather whatever supplies they'd need at the small convenience store that serviced the RV park just behind. He would then only need to make the trip to Coeur D'Alene once a month for items the convenience store did not carry.

Inside the store, Jed grabbed a small cart and headed down each aisle, gathering toiletries, cleaning supplies, and food. He avoided eye contact with other shoppers, mostly tourists staying in the RV park, and completed the chore as quickly as he could. At the register he placed each item on the counter then removed his wallet as the clerk rang up the bill.

The clerk, a twenty-something with long hair pulled into a ponytail and a spotty beard, bagged the merchandise carefully. Midway through he glanced at Jed. "You live up in the forest don't you?"

"Yup."

"Eric, right?"

Jed glanced at him. He still wasn't used to being known as Eric Bingsley, the pseudonym the relocation agent had given him.

"You had to show your ID last week when you bought that cough medicine."

"Yeah. Right."

The clerk finished bagging the items and punched a button on the register. "Fifty-nine, thirty-four."

As Jed removed three twenties from his wallet, the clerk said, "Where you from?"

Jed took quick inventory of the store. There was a woman by the frozen section, mid-fifties, short, thin; a teenage male checking out the magazine rack, flipping through a Sports Illustrated; a man, forties, thick build, full beard, reading the label on a box of cereal. The man glanced at Jed then went back to whatever interested him on that label.

"East," Jed said. He wanted to get out of there. He suddenly felt he needed to.

"How far east?" The clerk opened the register and removed some coins. "I've been to Ohio but that's as far east as I've been."

Jed put out his hand. He remained calm, not wanting to raise suspicion from the clerk or the other shoppers. "All the way. East coast." He'd been in the store three other times and not once had this cashier or any other attempted to engage him in conversation.

"I've never been to the east coast," the clerk said. "I've never been to any coast, never stood on a beach. Crazy, huh?"

Jed looked again to the bearded man, who was now reading the label on a box of instant oatmeal. Pocketing the change, he said to the clerk, "Yeah, crazy. You'll have to get there sometime. Thanks." He grabbed his bags and exited the store.

Outside, the storm front had crept closer, now breaching the edge of the Coeur D'Alene basin. The air was oddly still.

Getting in his truck, Jed glanced back at the store. The bearded man was at the counter now. He said something to the cashier who then turned to look at Jed.

Jed hesitated, vacillating between an urge to go back into the store and confront the men, find out what they were saying, what they knew, and scolding himself for being so paranoid. The clerk might have just been making light conversation in an attempt to be friendly. It certainly wasn't uncommon for the area. And the bearded man may have just been a nosey local or a curious tourist. Nothing sinister, nothing dangerous.

But there was always the other possibility, the one Jed kept in the back of his mind but within easy reach. The possibility that they'd been found. Anything out of the ordinary, any daily event that seemed unusual, stirred in him the awareness that his nightmare had become a reality. And a bearded forty-something checking out the label on a box of cereal was out of the ordinary.

The road through the Coeur D'Alene National Forest followed the winding curves of Hayden Creek deep into the dense land of trees. Hemlock, Douglas-fir, spruce, and lodgepole pines all towered above the road, spreading their needled branches like umbrellas, protecting the earth from the falling rays of the sun. Eventually, near Crooked Ridge, the road divided and Jed steered the pick-up onto a dirt service road that would lead him all the way to Chico Mountain.

The road wound for miles like a snake weaving through a wheat field. Jed wondered what it would be like to make his weekly trek out of the forest in the dead of winter. He was sure he'd be glad he had the Silverado.

At times, in higher elevations, the forest thinned to reveal craggy rock formations jutting from the earth's crust like rotted half-broken teeth.

Near the summit of Chico Mountain another dirt road split from the service road. It was this trail that would take Jed another mile into the forest and back to the cabin, back to Karen and Lilly.

Finally, in the clearing where the cabin sat, Jed stopped the truck and killed the engine. He sat in the silence of the cab for a moment, waiting. It was odd that Karen and Lilly weren't there to greet him. They usually heard the Silverado's large tires crunching dirt as it approached the clearing and met him at the truck. But today the clearing remained quiet and still.

Something was wrong. Prickles danced on the back of Jed's neck, his heart rate quickened. He drew in a deep breath. It could be nothing. Maybe they'd gone for a hike or to collect fire wood. But they never strayed far from the cabin. They still would have heard him approaching.

Jed reached across the seat and retrieved a hand gun. Slowly, he opened the truck's door and stepped out, listening, watching.

The clearing was as still as any postcard photo. The headwinds of the approaching storm had yet to reach the top of Chico Mountain. On all sides the forest stretched as far as the eye could see. Varying shades of green coated the terrain like a bristly blanket. To the west that storm front loomed, closer. It was moving slowly but relentlessly. Inching nearer, threatening to let loose the fury of heaven on the basin and forest. It had overtaken the city of Coeur D'Alene and now neared the edge of the national forest. If

Karen and Lilly were in the woods, if they'd ventured too far and gotten lost, he would need to find them quickly before the elements struck, unleashing nature's ferocity on them without the protection of shelter.

But one glance at the cabin told another story. The front door was ajar. Whether inside or outside, Karen would not leave it open; she was deathly afraid of giving some mountain-dwelling rodent or worse, a cougar or bear, free entry into their living space to set up a home of its own.

Heart now in his throat, pulse pounding through his neck, and gripping the gun with both hands, Jed crossed the distance between the truck and mounted the steps, then pushed the door open with his foot.

The interior of the cabin appeared untouched, as if Karen and Lilly had left and simply forgot to close the door. Maybe Karen had instructed Lilly to close it and like any nine-year-old she'd gotten distracted, maybe by a bird or a chipmunk or a rabbit, and failed to do so. Or maybe . . . *God, please no.*

Slowly, Jed moved farther into the cabin, gun still raised, expecting an intruder to reveal himself at any moment and squeeze off a shot or attack with some other kind of weapon. Jed listened as he stepped through the room. His first warning would be the sound of movement. Clothes rustling, floorboard creaking, a sudden exhale. He needed to stay alert, focused, and ready to react with only a fraction of a second's warning.

The cabin only had two bedrooms and Jed first checked Lilly's. The door to her room was already open. He entered and paced the floor, sweeping the handgun back and forth and always listening. When he had cleared the room he then moved to second bedroom. The door was closed here but Karen usually kept it closed. She had at their other home too, the one where the men had intruded, hunted Jed, and met early deaths. The home where Jed discovered things about himself that both awed and terrified him.

At the bedroom, he put his hand on the doorknob and turned slowly. When the knob was fully turned and the latch fully disengaged, he quickly shoved open the door and stepped through, gun high and ready to spit bullets.

But there were no masked men hiding in the closet or under the bed, no armed assassins waiting behind the door. Only a solitary figure crouched in the corner. Karen.

When she saw Jed, she sprang to her feet and threw herself into his arms. The tears came quickly as sobs wracked her frame.

Jed held her with one arm while keeping the handgun ready for action with the other. He still hadn't cleared the rest of the cabin.

"Karen, what happened here? Where's Lilly?" Even as the question exited his mouth a rock dropped into the pit of his stomach. Lilly wasn't there.

Jed pulled Karen away and held her at arm's length. Tears stained her cheeks and matted hair to her face. "Karen, where's Lilly?"

She dragged the back of her hand across her face. "They took her. Jed, they took our baby girl."

It is important to note that when using third person POV with multiple POV characters you only use one POV character per scene. This allows the reader to

63

be immersed in one character's world for the entire scene without having to jump back and forth between characters. To switch POV characters in a scene is called "head-hopping."

Here's an example of head-hopping:

> John reached for Diane's hand. "Here, take it. I don't bite."
> Diane took his hand in hers and squeezed. John's hand was firm and warm. She'd never held a boys hand before. Her heart thumped in her chest and she wondered if John could hear it.
> A smiled touched John's mouth. He could feel Diane's racing pulse through the soft flesh of her fingers.

See what's happening in that scene? We're in both John's and Diane's head, experiencing what each of them think and feel.

Here's how the scene could be re-written to only be in John's POV:

> John reached for Diane's hand. "Here, take it. I don't bite."
> She hesitated then took his hand and squeezed. A tinge of pink shaded her cheeks.
> A smile touched John's mouth. He could feel Diane's racing pulse through the soft flesh of her fingers.

Now the scene is totally in John's POV. We can still convey the shyness of Diane through the blushing and racing pulse but we stay in John's head.

It's of utmost importance to get this POV thing right. Before every scene determine who the POV character will be (in first person this will be easy!) then stay in that person's head. The rule of thumb with POV is that you can only write what the POV character would be able to sense or think/feel. You cannot write about something happening "off screen" in another area that the POV character would not be able to see or know about. You cannot include information the POV character would have no knowledge of. You cannot write, *What John didn't know . . .* Because if John didn't or couldn't know it, you can't write it. You as the writer, and by default the reader as well, are stuck inside the POV character's head and body. Insert yourself there and only write what the POV character can see, smell, hear, taste, feel, think, or experience in any other way.

This is why first person is so difficult. The entire story can only be told through one person's eyes and experiences. My suggestion to new writers is to always use third person until you master the use of POV. Then branch out into first person.

Before we go on to tenses we need to discuss internal dialogue. Internal dialogue is a technique used in deep third person POV to allow the reader to know what a character is thinking and feeling. It's the narrator, speaking as the POV character, revealing thoughts to the reader. For instance, here's an excerpt from chapter two of my novel, *Kill Devil*:

> Rage like he'd not felt before, or at least could not remember
> feeling, boiled beneath Jed's skin. Now his hands trembled. How?
> How could they have found his family?

He cupped Karen's face in his hands. Her eyes were red and swollen; her lips trembled.

Jed tried to calm his voice. She was already a wreck; he'd only make things worse if he showed his anger and panic. "Karen, who took her? Who, huh?"

"Men." She sniffed, ran the palm of her hand across her nose.

Jed rubbed his thumbs over her cheeks, wiping the tears. His mind spun in a thousand different directions. He was already in planning mode, formulating a strategy to retrieve his daughter. "What men? How many?"

"There were three of them. They had guns. They . . . they said they were coming back for me."

"What did they want? Why did they take Lilly?"

Karen sniffed again and licked her lips. "They wanted the thumb drive."

The drive. It contained every damaging piece of information about the Centralia Project. It named names, pointed fingers, implicated politicians at the very highest levels. It would be the shockwave of the century, a scandal that would be talked and read about for decades to come. It'd been almost four weeks since Lawrence Habit had handed it to Jed and he'd done nothing with it. He would; he planned to. But he needed to make sure his family was safe first. And he wanted time to get to know them again, to bond and laugh and cry with them; to love them. Once he took steps to get the drive into the right hands he knew their road would grow rough again.

He wanted to make sure it happened on his terms, though, and in the time of his choosing.

But he never got to make that choice. The roughened road had found him and now forced him to walk it once again.

"They thought I had it," she said. "Or knew where it was."

But she didn't. Jed had buried it in a small metal box outside the cabin at the edge of the clearing. The location was marked with a formation of softball-sized rocks.

Jed pulled his wife close and pressed her head against his chest. She began to sob again.

"It's all right," he said, stroking her hair. But it wasn't. None of this was all right. He now cursed himself for not taking action with the thumb drive sooner. He'd been selfish and now it had come back to bite him.

Outside, rain began to fall. Large drops pelted the roof of the cabin like hundreds of fingers drumming at once.

But how could they have found him? The only ones who knew their location were Habit and Roger Abernathy. And to his knowledge, they both perished helping Jed, Karen, and Lilly escape from the Centralia paramilitary forces.

Notice how Jed's thoughts are written as narrative. The narrator and Jed are one, they are the same person. The narrator is inside Jed's mind allowing the reader to read what Jed is thinking and feeling.

Internal dialogue is crucial to allowing the reader to make a very strong connection to your characters.

Now, a word about tenses. There are two tenses that you will write fiction in: present tense and past tense. The vast majority of fiction is written in the past tense. Occasionally, you will find a novel or short story written in present tense. Again, I suggest the beginning fiction writer focus on past tense. This comes the most naturally to us because it's typically the way we tell stories and recount events that happened to us.

Here's a version of our example above with John and Diane written in present tense:

> John reaches for Diane's hand. "Here, take it. I don't bite."
> She hesitates then takes his hand and squeezes. A tinge of pink shades her cheeks.
> A smile touches John's mouth. He can feel Diane's racing pulse through the soft flesh of her fingers.

And here is the same scene in first person, past tense:

> I reached for Diane's hand. "Here, take it. I don't bite."
> She hesitated then took my hand and squeezed. A tinge of pink shaded her cheeks.
> A smile touched my mouth. I could feel Diane's racing pulse through the soft flesh of her fingers.

Here it is in first person, present tense:

> I reach for Diane's hand. "Here, take it. I don't bite."
>
> She hesitates then takes my hand and squeezes. A tinge of pink shades her cheeks.
>
> A smile touches my mouth. I can feel Diane's racing pulse through the soft flesh of her fingers.

And just for fun, here it is in second person, present tense:

> You reach for Diane's hand. "Here, take it. I don't bite."
>
> She hesitates then takes your hand and squeezes. A tinge of pink shades her cheeks.
>
> A smile touches your mouth. You can feel Diane's racing pulse through the soft flesh of her fingers.

See the difference of each? And each has a different feel to it. So how do you determine which POV and tense to use for your story? There is no formula for which POV and tense to use. It comes down to how you want to tell the story and how you want the story to feel to the reader. I can tell you that most fiction is written in third person, past tense. But that doesn't mean all fiction has to be written like that. For beginners it's what I recommend but please, feel free to experiment. It comes down to asking yourself this question: How does this story want to be told? When you become intimate with your story idea you'll get a good feeling for how it wants to be told.

Generally speaking, first person is going to be very intimate. The reader is solely focused on the protagonist and her life/situation/ordeal/story. Third person can be intimate as well but it allows for other POVs to enter into the story. Past tense is most comfortable for readers; it's what we are used to the most. But that doesn't mean you can't experiment with present tense. Present tense usually works well for short stories or flash fiction (What's flash fiction? See the appendix) or sometimes isolated scenes in a novel (for instance, the novel may be written in past tense for every character but the antagonist who gets present tense scenes).

A final note on POV. People are different. We speak differently than those around us, think differently, act differently. Your characters should be different too. The way you write their POV scenes should reflect their unique personality. This is why it's important to think about who the character is, maybe do a biographical sketch for each character. Think about his or her personality, likes, dislikes, quirks, world view. Think about how they treat others. Is she a natural leader? Is he a follower? Is he outspoken or quiet and timid? All this will play into the way the scene is written from that character's POV. Imagine you are that character and tell her story from her perspective (this works for both first person and third person, by the way).

If you can practice and get this POV thing right your readers will love your characters and they will praise your work.

Additional Reading:

Writer's Digest: "Fiction: Point of View" http://www.writersdigest.com/writing-articles/by-writing-goal/write-first-chapter-get-started/fiction-point-of-view

She's Novel: "How to Write in Deep POV and Get Inside the Mind of Your Character" http://www.shesnovel.com/blog/how-to-write-in-deep-pov

Your Turn:

Assignment 1: Write a scene in third person, past tense using what you've learned so far about dialogue, setting, and description. Include some dialogue, some action, and description of setting. Make sure to write it from one character's POV. (at l

east 500 words)

Assignment 2: Re-write the scene from Assignment 1 so it is in first person, past tense. Then re-write it again so it is in first person, present tense.

Section 5

SETTING

Setting gives your story context, it provides texture. Without setting your story is a few characters on an empty stage with no props, no background. It's vacant. Boring. We live in a world of setting. Everywhere we go there are things: buildings, streets, vehicles, trees, rocks, valleys, mountains. We feel the environment around us, the temperature, humidity level, precipitation. There are landmarks, historical sites, terrain changes. There is stuff. Our fictional world should be no different. Our characters need a world to live in, they need setting. A house to live in, cars to drive, roads to drive on, sidewalks to walk down, forests to hike through, mountains to climb, oceans to swim.

When you create the setting for your story spend significant time thinking about the mood of each scene. Setting is so much more than a conglomeration of props thrown onto the page. It's almost like an additional character that has a personality of its own.

Think about each scene and determine how the setting will play a role in determining the mood of that scene. Will it take place in the woods? What kind of shadows are there? What noises are heard? What's on the forest floor? Can you see the sun through the canopy? What time of day is it? Or maybe the scene takes place in a building? What kind of building? What kind of shape is the building in? Are there other people in the building? Where is the building located? All these issues and more need to be determined and each will play a major role in setting the mood and feel for the scene.

Also, think about how the characters will interact with the setting. Are they just walking through? Are they planted there for an extended period of time? Are they talking, kissing, fighting? And think about how the setting will interact with the characters. Does it aid them or hinder them? Does it provide conflict or ease tensions?

One other thing regarding setting. It doesn't matter whether you base the location(s) of your story in a real place or a fictional place. But do research. If it's a real place, either visit that location if you can or do much research (Google is great for this). I almost always check out the place on Google Maps so I get street names right and get a feel for the layout of the location. You can research landmarks, terrain, flora and fauna, popular places, roads and highways. It's all there at your fingertips. With the technology we have now days you can sit in your living room and virtually visit a location and get a real good feel for it. But, that being said, there's nothing quite like visiting the place itself. Which is why I place many of my novels in southern Pennsylvania, Maryland, or northern Virginia. I'm familiar with those locales. Or, I place my stories in places I've visited.

In this scene in *Fear Mountain* notice how the setting is described and how it plays into the mood of the moment. It's described almost as if it's another character in and of itself.

73

As I stepped outside, I drew in a deep breath of the cool air. It was full of the musky scent of dirt and pine and decomposing leaves. It was cold but not bitterly, enough though to tighten my skin. Above us, the early morning sky was murky black, and I could no sooner separate the ink-stained woodland canopy from the vacant universe beyond as I could differentiate between Martians from Mars and those from the dark side of the nomadic moon.

Our cabin sits in a small clearing on the side of Bear Mountain in western Maine, miles from anything that could even remotely be considered civilized. Eons ago, long before I was born, long before even Pop was born, a local hunter got lost on the mountain and was presumed dead and gone. Three weeks later he appeared, dehydrated, half-starved, filthy, and confused. The story goes that as he stumbled back into civilization he kept mumbling something about surviving Fear Mountain. The name stuck with the locals and the peak has been called such ever since. The closest town to Bear Mountain is the village of Woodsmall, ten miles down route 34, and route 34 is a good five miles down the mountain, if you are a crow. If not, the drive along the rutted and winding service road as it snakes its way down Bear Mountain is no less than seven or eight miles. And Woodsmall, though officially designated a village, is hardly that. It consists of eleven homes (twelve if you count the O'Malley's oversized and ostentatious dog house for their black lab, Duke), one barbershop, one farm supply store, and one grocery with an ice cream parlor.

Bear Mountain rises out of miles and miles of patchworked farmland and forest dotted with villages no larger than Woodsmall.

We live on a 100-acre farm ten miles from Woodsmall. Someday I plan to leave the farm and travel the country, preaching the good news of God's Word.

Looking up into the abyss that sprawled above us, watching the darkness enclose and swallow the flashlight's beam much like an octopus envelopes its prey in a tangle of tentacles and slowly, steadily, draws the helpless victim toward its beaklike mouth, I realized how suffocating a moonless night really was, as if the sky were an eight-armed predator and we its helpless prey. I closed the cabin door behind me and huddled close to Henry. After all, he was the one with the shotgun and if something sinister and violence-craved with a beak for a mouth was waiting for us, I'd much rather him pull the trigger than me try to blind it with my flashlight.

We both stood still for a minute or two, quieting our breathing, listening. I heard nothing. Not the rustle of leaves as a gentle breeze played in their branches, not the crunch of pine needles as wildlife foraged for food or buried treasure, not the hooting of an owl, not even the high-pitched chirp of a bat. The morning was eerily silent and still. I thought of the lost hunter all those years ago and his ramblings about Fear Mountain.

I ran the beam of the light over the tree line, back and forth. The light highlighted the massive trunks of ancient oaks and maples, sycamores, walnut, and white spruce, but did nothing to illumine the forest behind them. It reminded me of plays I'd seen where the cast, illuminated by several strategically placed spotlights, is back-dropped by a thick black curtain.

Keeping my voice to a whisper so any beaked, tentacled,

rapacious carnivores lurking behind the curtain, off-stage, wouldn't hear, I said, "Where are they? I don't see them."

And here's another example of how setting can be personified with description.

We approached the house with all the caution we would if it were a living, breathing thing, an animal in the wild, maybe a lion. Padding from tree to tree, we used the density of the woods to conceal ourselves.

The sun was an orange, swollen disc and well into its downward arc by now, almost touching the horizon. Sunset comes early on the eastern side of the mountain. Nightfall would not be a friend to us.

When we reached the clearing I got a better look at the house. Someone's seasonal hunting cabin it was not. With two stories, a cellar, and an expansive front porch, it was at least as large as our farmhouse. The architecture was sharp and straightforward, unpretentious like our house. Asbestos siding wrapped the house in a green cloak, the glass in the windows was bubbled and wavy, and a thick layer of moss covered the eastern side of the slate shingled roof. The white paint on the porch and window framing was blistered and peeling, like the house had a bad case of sunburn. Two of the steps leading to the porch were obviously rotted, the boards having been offered up as a peace offering to a horde of pitiless termites. A deeply rutted, partially overgrown lane wove in from the far side of the woods and ended next to the outside cellar doors. No lights illuminated the windows. There were no automobiles parked outside, no horses or sign of horses anywhere nearby. The place appeared abandoned.

Think about some of your favorite stories, either movies or books, and how setting played a role in creating the mood for the story. Think about how the characters interacted with the setting and how the setting influenced the characters. Setting is very important!

Additional Reading:

Writer's Digest: "Discover the Basic Elements of Setting in a Story"

http://www.writersdigest.com/tip-of-the-day/discover-the-basic-elements-of-setting-in-a-story

Author's Craft: "Narrative Elements: Setting"

http://udleditions.cast.org/craft_elm_setting.html

Now Novel: "How to Write a Book: Setting"

http://www.nownovel.com/blog/talking-setting-place/

Your Turn:

Assignment 1: Spend ten minutes outside and record everything you see and hear, down to the smallest detail. We often overlook those minor subtleties. Record what you see: trees, roadways, sidewalks, houses, buildings, birds, other animals, etc. Don't miss a thing. Be very observant and get it all down on paper.

Assignment 2: Describe the setting for a scene using what you recorded in Assignment 1. Create a three-dimensional setting for the character to live in.

Don't describe the exact scene, but rather use what you recorded to create an entirely new setting. Be as creative as you want. (at least 400 words)

DIALOGUE

Dialogue is one of the aspects of fiction writing that most novice writers struggle with the most. It's difficult to get it right. Too often, writers want to write dialogue the way they think it should sound rather than the way it really sounds. Dialogue is one of those things that is with us every day but we rarely actually pay attention to it. We hear people talk all day but it's so commonplace our brains don't pick up on the nuances of how those words are formed, how sentences are formed, and the way people put those words and sentences into dialogue.

Want to know how to improve your ability to write great dialogue? Listen to people talk. Don't just hear them, but listen. Listen to the way they sound, the words they use, the way they form sentences. Listen to the rhythm of conversations, how two people banter with dialogue.

It's not what you think. It rarely follows the rules of grammar. And people speak in sentence fragments all the time.

Here are a few things to keep in mind when writing dialogue.

Each character should have his or her own way of talking, distinct from the other characters in the story. I sound different than you when I talk. I have favorite words or phrases I use. I may pronounce words differently. The rhythm of my dialogue will be different than the rhythm of your dialogue. We are different people so we talk differently. In the same manner, your character's language and dialogue should be unique to him or her. You don't want a cast of characters who all sound the same. That's boring for the reader.

Dialogue as a whole should always move the story forward. Yes, there may be normal, mundane words exchanged, but in the end, the conversation must be purposeful. It must share some new information or show something new about the personality or values of the character. It must mean something to the story as a whole.

Dialogue attributions should be kept to he said/she said or he asked/she asked as much as possible. Try to avoid using attributions like *he quipped* or *she snapped*. And use adverbs in attributions very sparingly (example: he said wryly). The context and tone of the dialogue itself should convey the emotion behind the words. This isn't easy to do but can be mastered with practice and listening. When possible, avoid attributions altogether and show who the speaker is by actions.

For instance: Jake rubbed his chin thoughtfully. "I'm sorry. I have to disagree with just about everything you just said."

Intersperse action with dialogue. Nobody stands stock still while having a conversation with another person. We move, we scratch, we shift our weight, we get distracted by what's going on around us, we run our hands through our hair or tuck loose strands of hair behind our ear. We do things. We move. Show the reader that your characters are not cardboard cutouts with movable mouths. They are real people engaged in a real conversation.

Read this scene from *Fear Mountain* and notice how dialogue is handled and interspersed with description and action:

"Missing." I dropped the flashlight a little so the beam now highlighted Dad's thighs and knees. "What do you mean, *missing?*"

Dad lowered his brow and pressed his lips into a thin line. He shifted his eyes from me to Henry then back to me again then let them fall to the ground. "Boys, Pop's got oldtimers disease. He was diagnosed a few months back by Doc Richards. Said he's not a hundred percent sure but all the ways Pop's been acting lately says it is."

I looked over at Henry, not sure if he knew what Dad was talking about. The confused look on his face confirmed my suspicion. "Alzheimer's," I said, then wished I hadn't. Somehow, Dad's "oldtimers" seemed less sinister, less final, less vicious. There's not a lot known about Alzheimer's, its cause and cure, but one thing that is known is that it's brutal, merciless. Like a cunning con man, it slowly robs its host of his memories, stealing the one thing he thought could never be taken from him. And what it leaves is a shell of the person you once knew, a hollowed out flesh and blood shell. The person inside is lost forever, like Pop wandering in the woods with no idea where he was.

Henry gave me a blank look that said more than he ever could have in words. He bounced the butt of the shotgun on the ground. "What's that got to do with him missing?"

"Alzheimer's is a disease that slowly eats away at a person's brain. They slowly lose their mind. You know we've been kidding Pop about his forgetfulness for years, and how he tells you the same thing every time you see him."

I couldn't believe I hadn't seen the symptoms before now. Thinking about it and saying it out loud made it all so real. I could have diagnosed him months, maybe years ago.

"One symptom is wandering," I said, "especially at night. The person will just wander off and not know where he's going or why he's going there. Sometimes they realize later what they've done, sometimes they don't."

The thought of Pop roaming the woods at this hour twisted my stomach into a knot. He wasn't lost and looking to be found, he was just lost. And didn't even know he was lost. A new sense of urgency came over me then. We needed to find him before he hurt himself. Or got hurt by something else. I didn't even want to think about the wildlife—bears, coyotes, bobcats—that also roamed these woods at night.

"Eventually, he won't even recognize us, won't remember the memories we've shared, won't even remember his own name. His mind will be a blank slate, an empty box."

Tears pooled in my eyes and blurred the image of Dad and

82

Henry. Both glanced at the tree line, and I took the opportunity to swipe at the wetness now on my cheek. It's unthinkable how an entire lifetime of living and feeling and loving and *experiencing* can be erased, obliterated, expunged, as if the life had never been lived. You go through life storing up images and names and memories of every variety in hopes that when you've come full circle and you've lost your ability to see or hear or taste or walk that at least, *at the very least*, you'll have your memories. *People can rob you of anything and everything . . . except your mind,* I once heard someone say. But your mind can be robbed and though everyone around you may remember that you lived, as far as you're concerned, they never existed, their lives were only vapors, appearing as a mist then gone with no memory or residue of a life lived, well or otherwise. Alzheimer's was an awful beast, a devil of a disease, a merciless thief of life.

"It's my fault," Dad said, his voice thick. "Should have never brought him here. I thought maybe being out here at his cabin, in the woods, hunting, would jog his memory. He told me a few weeks back that he couldn't remember ever hunting. Asked me if he'd ever shot anything."

Pop was one of the greatest hunters in Maine. A legend. Everyone from the western farming land to the central woodland to the coastal region had heard the name Elmer Harding at least once. Harding and hunting were synonymous. Had he ever shot anything? Only more buck than any other hunter in the state, more bear than I could count on two hands, and more moose than most whole towns saw in a lifetime. And he shot more than wildlife too. Pop served as an officer in World War I and came home with a breast full of polished medals.

Dad continued, "I heard him get out of bed, heard the cot creak. By the time I was fully awake and knew what was happening, he was out the door. At first I thought maybe he was just going outside to pee, you know how he is, then I saw he'd left behind his slippers and boots. He'd never do that. That's when I knew he was wandering off again. Gram said he's done it maybe four, five times already. I grabbed my gun and ran outside, even forgot my flashlight, but he was gone that quickly. I didn't even think, just went tearing into the woods looking for him."

"So what, Pop's got some bug in his head?" Henry asked in all sincerity.

He was looking at me as I had unwittingly established myself as the resident Alzheimer's expert. "Bugs?" I questioned.

"You said something's eating away at Pop's brain. Isn't there some medicine or something Doc Richards can give him to kill it?"

Apparently, my description of the disease's unpitying and relentless attack on the brain cells led my brother to believe Alzheimer's was a living, breathing creature not unlike the meningeal worm that plants itself inside the cranium of deer or sheep, spreads out its picnic blanket, and enjoys a smorgasbord of gray and white matter.

"Alzheimer's isn't a bug," I said. "It's not alive, it's just a disease. No one really knows what it is."

Looking like a student who didn't fully trust his teacher's claim that sightings of eight-foot hairy hominoids in the Texas forestland were nothing but some drunk hunter's imagination or his ill-shaven, overweight cousin, Henry said, "So they *could* be bugs."

I shook my head. "I don't think so. I'm sure they've done autopsies on people who've died with Alzheimer's and they would've found the bugs then."

Henry shrugged and turned his eyes toward the tree line.

I glanced at Dad. "Did you hear the moan?"

Dad nodded and looked directly into my eyes. He was an authoritative man, the dominant type, and the weight of his stare always made me cower just a little. "Yeah. But it didn't sound like him."

I shook my head, brushed the hair off my forehead. "No it didn't. It came from over there—" I pointed behind me at the trees standing like sentries, guarding the woods and whatever secrets it held, "—then there." I showed him where the last moan was heard, at a forty-five degree angle from where we stood. "He—the sound—was moving."

"Let me get my flashlight and we'll split up, look for him."

Dad disappeared into the cabin, leaving Henry and me standing alone outside. My brother's quietness told me he was troubled. Henry is not a talkative person by nature, but he's not an introvert either . . . except when he's upset about something. Then, like a turtle, he pulls into his shell and folds up within himself, not letting anyone see the hurt that is eating away at him. I'm not sure why he does that, whether because he just can't find the words to express himself or because he's too proud, too tough on the exterior, to show the softness that hides behind the shell. Exposing his belly, his soft spot, would be too vulnerable for him. Dad's like that too. So is Aaron.

While we waited, I asked Henry, "You okay?"

He nodded, but didn't look at me. I watched his Adam's apple bob with some difficulty in his throat and knew he was battling the same lump I was. "I'm fine. We just need to find—"

From somewhere deep in the woods, still to our left, the moan came again, crawling over the leaves, slithering between the trees, into our clearing. It was low and prolonged this time, lasting maybe three, four seconds. A chill, like a cold hand, raced down my spine and settled at the top of my buttocks when the recognition came: it was the sound of pain, the moan associated with great grief or agony, when words fail and the only sound that can escape a tightened jaw and clenched teeth is from somewhere deep in the throat, from the soul. I pictured Pop lying on the ground, ankle twisted at an odd angle, too frightened and injured to holler or shout, able only to expel a pained groan. Then an image, unbidden, flashed through my mind of Pop being dragged by the back of the neck by some angry bear or pack of coyotes, or, God forbid, an eight-foot, hairy ape-man, dragged off to some remote location where he'd be eviscerated and eaten alive. I closed my eyes hard and pushed the gruesome image from my head.

Henry must have recognized the moan too. He nearly dropped his gun and ran into the cabin. "Dad, let's go. We heard it again."

Dad came barreling out of the cabin like a steam engine, breathing hard, clutching his gun in one hand, the flashlight in the other. He swept the beam of light back and forth over the tree line. The sight of those trunks, pushing up from the ground and standing

86

immovable for decades, probably centuries, made me think of giants. And I knew we'd be crossing the border, trespassing into their land, walking among them.

"We need to split up," Dad said. "I'll go that way—" he pointed the flashlight to our immediate left, where we first heard the moan, "—and you two go that way." He pointed in front of us, in front of the cabin. "We'll go out maybe a hundred, hundred and fifty yards, then move toward each other. He's gotta be somewhere in that area."

"We'll find him," Henry said, trying his hardest to sound confident and brave like Dad. I could tell he was scared, though, maybe even as much as I was.

We watched as Dad and his light faded into the trees, then we walked forward, huddled closer than we needed to be, me with my trusty light and Henry with his shotgun.

With one step we left the mottled, dry grass of the clearing and entered the land of the goliaths and a world of unknowns.

Additional Reading:

Nathan Bransford: "Seven Keys to Writing Good Dialogue"

http://blog.nathanbransford.com/2010/09/seven-keys-to-writing-good-dialogue.html

Standout Books: "6 Insanely Good Dialogue Tips From Your Future Literary Agent" https://www.standoutbooks.com/6-insanely-good-dialogue-tips-from-your-future-literary-agent/

Your Turn:

Assignment 1: Screenplays and teleplays must be strong in dialogue and are a great reference for learning how to write effective dialogue in fiction. Watch a television show or movie and choose a conversation between two characters to transcribe. This will be easier with a show/movie where you can pause the action. Write out every word. Don't worry about attributions or action or anything else. Just write the spoken words. Then read carefully what you wrote. Notice the back and forth of the conversation; notice how words are used and how the dialogue flows. (choose a conversation that will give you at least 100 words of dialogue)

Assignment 2: Write a conversation between two characters. Add in some conflict. Include attributions (used sparingly) and action/description. (at least 400 words)

Section 7

PACING

Pacing is important in a story because it directly relates to the "feel" of a story. And remember, so much of fiction writing is about creating a feeling in the reader. There are slow-paced stories and fast-paced stories. You want your story to be somewhere in the middle. You want your reader to feel like she is on a roller coaster. Slow, fast, slow, fast. Nobody likes a roller coaster that just crawls along the whole ride. It's boring, uneventful. There's nothing to keep your attention or make you want to talk about it afterwards. On the other hand, a roller coaster that goes a hundred miles an hour the entire time is also a little much. It's overkill. And it feels like it ends way too soon. The ups and downs of a roller coaster, the pace changes, is what keeps it interesting, makes it exciting. There is anticipation created, thrills, and time to catch your breath.

A novel should be like a good roller coaster. There will be times when the story races along and the scenes are full of action, and there should be times when the action slows and the reader can take a break. The slower scenes are when you, the author, catch the reader up on information. Usually there is more dialogue in these scenes, both internal and external.

There are a few easy ways to manipulate the pacing of your story.

One, a general rule of thumb: short sentences and paragraphs make the story feel like it's moving faster. This applies to dialogue as well. Short, choppy dialogue moves much quicker than long, drawn out monologues. This is an easy way to pick up the pace. It will usually happen during action scenes.

Two, strong verbs move the action forward at breakneck speed. For instance . . .

Eric balled his hand and slammed his attacker in the jaw moves faster than *Eric punched his attacker in the jaw.*

Three, use slower scenes to get the reader caught up on important information. Fast-paced scenes won't inform the reader much. Mostly, they are used for fleshing out the plot, for moving things forward physically. Slow-paced scenes are used to convey information to the reader. Here, the dialogue may move slower and be more substantive. There will be more information included.

Four, use cliffhangers to keep readers reading. Cliffhangers are when you end a chapter or scene with unfinished business. They create in the reader a desire to read on to find out what happens. Sometimes cliffhangers will be very dramatic, like leaving the protagonist literally dangling over the edge of a cliff. At other times they will be subtler but still create in the reader a sense of mystery, a need to read on and find out how the action or conflict resolves.

Here's an example of a cliffhanger from *Fear Mountain:*

Henry's left eye fluttered open. "I'm here, Billy. I'm listening."

His pulse thumped through his carotid, faster than it should have been. Looking him over, tears sprung to my eyes, and a sob threatened to jump out of my throat. I wondered why the Germans hadn't beaten me like they did Henry. Was it because he'd put up a fight, like any proud American should, and I rolled over like a dog assuming the submissive posture? Or was it because they just hadn't gotten around to me yet and my quality time with my new friends was still on the horizon? Maybe tonight. Maybe tomorrow. I could hear their muffled voices on the first floor. Loud talking, then laughter, then hushed tones, then more laughter. On and on it went.

Henry's eye closed again and he took a deep, ragged breath that shuddered in his chest.

"Henry," I said. "Come on brother, hang on, okay? Just hang on. I'm gonna get us out of here."

Even as I spoke the last word, the sound of heavy boots ascending the stairs made my heart shiver behind its bony bars.

Notice how the chapter ends with unfinished business. The reader is left anticipating what is going to happen next. He feels like he has to turn to the next chapter to find out.

Additional Reading:

*(This is a great article) Fiction Factor: "Pacing"

http://www.fictionfactor.com/guests/pacing.html

Cheryl Reif Writes: "How to Write Cliffhanger Chapter Endings" http://www.cherylreif.com/2015/02/23/cliffhanger-chapter-ends/ (note: there is one instance of swearing in this article but I didn't want to omit the whole article because of it)

Your Turn:

Write a short, fast-paced scene that ends with a cliffhanger. Use the techniques described above to move the scene forward quickly then end it abruptly so the reader feels like she needs to keep reading to find out what happens next. Pay attention to sentence/paragraph lengths, strong action verbs, and that all-important cliffhanger. (at least 700 words)

FINAL PROJECT INFORMATION IS LOCATED AT THE END OF THE BOOK

MIKE

EARLY SIGNS

DELL

A JED PATRICK SHORT STORY

OSSO

The diner was like any other diner in northwestern Pennsylvania. Counter stools and vinyl-covered booth seats. Bright lighting, checkered tile floor. The smell of frying oil and a hot grill. It sat off Route 219, about seven miles south of Crenshaw and just a mile off I-80. Truckers liked it because it was convenient and cheap and had a large lot for them to park their big rigs in while they emptied their bladders and filled their stomachs while jawing about their many adventures on the road. Locals liked it because the service was good and the food was at least decent. And cheap.

The waitresses were like any you'd find in a truckstop diner along the open highway. Friendly, cute, skilled at anticipating a patron's needs, and right on time with a fresh cup of coffee.

Except one. She must have been a new hire. She was young, teenage, shapeless, plain, and appeared frazzled by the busyness of the dinner hour. She'd already mixed up one couple's order with another customer's. She'd dropped a dinner roll, splashed coffee on her uniform, and gave the wrong bill to the wrong trucker. He'd complained to the manager, who took the girl aside and gave her a stern finger-shaking.

So when Jedidiah Patrick saw the threesome of jocks enter the diner like they'd just won the state championship and find a booth in the back, in the new girl's section, he knew trouble would follow.

It started when she gave one of the guys Diet Coke instead of regular. He put up a fuss, asked her if she was new, then cracked some joke about how the diner was scraping the bottom of the barrel to find help. They all laughed. He was so funny. The girl blushed, took the soda, and returned a minute later with the regular Coke.

Jed didn't need this. He'd come to the diner to get away from Hank, his foster dad. Hank was not a violent or abusive man. He was, in fact, quite the opposite. Hank was a pacifist whose weapon of choice—in fact his only weapon—was his mouth. He liked to talk. He also liked to drink. Vodka. And when he drank he had a tendency to get very chatty and demonstrative about his views of the government. Conspiracy theories were his specialty. Sometimes Jed would listen out of politeness; sometimes he'd listen out of respect for Anna, his foster mother. She needed someone else in the house to buffer Hank's monologues and rants. He wondered if that's why Anna insisted on keeping a revolving door open for foster kids. But sometimes, Jed needed to get away. He needed some quiet to study, to do homework. It was his senior year and he wasn't about to flunk out now. Anna would have to handle Hank on her own.

The waitress returned to the table to take the jocks' orders. Jed could hear them from where he sat three booths away. Loudmouths. They kept changing their minds, asking all sorts of ridiculous questions about special ordering this and substituting that. Then, when she thought they were all set, one of them would change his order again. They'd all snicker and she'd blush an even brighter shade of red. She knew they were toying with her but she needed the job. Jed could tell by her worn sneakers.

Finally, they completed their order and the waitress left their table to check on another patron. But as she walked away one of the guys commented on a certain part of her anatomy. She paused, didn't look at them, blushed deeper still, then acted as if she hadn't heard the rude remark and took the empty plates from the next table.

Anger burned in Jed's chest. He closed his history textbook and clenched his fists. He'd been learning about the French Revolution. About Napoleon Bonaparte and King Louis XVI and Maximilien Robespierre. About the bourgeoisie and the constitution of 1791. Had a big test tomorrow that he needed to ace. The last thing he had time for was these punks stirring up trouble.

Ten minutes later the waitress returned with three plates and set them on the jocks' table.

"This isn't what I ordered," one of them said, his voice louder than it needed to be. He was trying to create a scene, draw attention to the waitress to embarrass and humiliate her further.

She tried to protest but the jerk interrupted. "Can't you get anything right? How long have you been working here?" He had very blonde hair that hung low, covered his forehead and part of his eye. He swept the hair off his face, then pushed the plate toward the edge of the table. "I don't want this garbage."

As the plate neared the edge the waitress reflexively lunged for it but in doing so succeeded only in knocking it off the table. The plate crashed to the floor, shattered into multiple pieces, and sent the burger and fries skittering along the tile.

"Look what you did now," Goldilocks hollered.

The waitress burst into tears and ran from the scene, which only prompted more laughter from the threesome.

A minute later another waitress appeared from the kitchen carrying a tray and a handful of towels. She was young and attractive. Jed had seen her before. She had a nice smile, warm and friendly, and her eyes always seemed bright and cheery. It was obvious that on most days she enjoyed her job. Moments like this, though, took the light from her eyes.

The waitress approached the table and the mess on the floor and got down on her knees to clean up the food.

"That's what I'm talkin' 'bout fellas," Goldilocks said. He made an obscene gesture which brought on a round of guffaws from his goon friends.

Jed didn't want to get involved. He really didn't. But this had gone too far. He couldn't sit there and allow jerks to get away with what came so naturally to them. And if no one else in the diner was going to intervene, then he would.

He slid out of his booth and approached the table and the waitress on the floor. "Miss, please stand up."

The waitress looked up at him with wide eyes. "It's okay." She nodded toward the trio. "I've dealt with worse. Besides, it's the end of my shift. I'm off in a couple minutes."

"But you shouldn't have to. Please. Get up."

"Who are you?" Goldilocks said.

The gorilla across the table from Goldilocks was a big guy, thick in the chest and arms, short hair on the sides, longer on top, spiked into a faux Mohawk. "Dude thinks he's superman," he said.

The waitress stood, holding the tray with the food and broken plate pieces on it. Jed said, "Can you get that other waitress out here, please? I think these guys owe her an apology."

"What?" Goldilocks scowled. "I ain't apologizin' to anybody!"

Jed kept his eyes on the punks but said again to the waitress, "Please? Can you get her?"

"She left," the waitress said. "Walked out."

Jed said, "That's a shame. I guess an apology to you will have to do."

"Man, you better get outta my face," Goldilocks said.

The guy next to Mohawk was smaller than the other two, wiry, and had a pocked face and a buzz cut. "Come on, fellas," he said. "Let's just get outta here. Food stinks anyway."

Mohawk tried to stand but Jed shoved him back into the booth. "Not 'til you apologize."

"Screw you," Goldilocks said. He, too, tried to push his way out of the booth but Jed sent him back into his seat with a fist to the mouth. Mohawk grabbed Jed's sleeve but Jed's reflexes were quick and he caught the guy in the jaw with the meaty side of his hand. Buzzcut lunged for Jed but he was trapped between Mohawk and the wall. He had nowhere to go.

Recovering from the shock of the hit he'd taken, Goldilocks swore loudly and took a swing at Jed, he missed but grabbed a fistful of Jed's shirt near the collar. He was stronger than he looked and pulled Jed down toward the table. Mohawk lifted a fork and jabbed it at Jed's face. But again, Jed was quicker and pulled away just enough to block the assault with his free arm. He then grabbed the back of Goldilock's head and rammed his face into the table. Goldilocks let go of Jed's shirt in time for Jed to deflect another blow by Mohawk and dislodge the fork from his hand. He then jammed his elbow into Mohawk's face and quickly shoved him against Buzzcut.

Jed turned to the waitress. Things were about to get ugly. "Let's go. We gotta get out of here."

"Agreed," she said. She placed the tray on the counter. Jeb grabbed his knapsack. As they left they passed the diner's owner. He stood behind the counter, wide-eyed and mouth agape. The waitress said, "Sorry, Carl. I'll call you later and explain everything."

As they exited the diner into the evening, Jed said, "You have a car?"

"Nope. I was going to walk home. Car's in the shop."

"Want a ride?"

"Are you asking me out?"

They reached Jed's Chevy Cavalier. "Not yet. Get in."

The waitress got in the passenger side as Jed slid behind the wheel. He turned the key and brought the engine to life. The Cavalier was a good car, solid and reliable. He'd bought it used with the money he'd saved from his part-time job at the auto shop. The job had allowed him to earn a few bucks during his senior year and gave him a few hours a week free of Hank and his unending rants about the evils of government.

A half-mile down the road, Jed said, "So what's your name?"

"Karen. Yours?"

"Jed. Who was that other waitress?"

"Sonya. She just started a few days ago. Poor girl. Had to get stuck with those idiots."

"You know them?"

"No. Sort of. They go to Brockway. They're all seniors and think they own the world."

"Not anymore." Outside the car, open fields skimmed past. A stand of trees stood just ahead. "Where do you live anyway?"

"Just down the road here you'll make a left at those trees. It's just a mile after that."

"And you walk this?"

"It's good exercise."

Jed glanced at the rearview mirror. "I can't take you home."

"You're not gonna go all creeper on me, are you? I have pepper spray on my keychain and I'm not afraid to use it."

"Nope. I'm not a creeper." He nodded at the mirror. "Look."

Karen turned in her seat and groaned. "The idiots."

"I can't let them know where you live."

"Yeah, I doubt they're very polite house guests."

Jed drove past the road where Karen had indicated she lived. "Where to?"

Karen shrugged. "We could head to town. Maybe they'll lay off in a public area."

Jed didn't like that option. "But they won't leave you alone. They know where you work and they now think you're with me."

"I am with you. I'm here, in your car."

Jed didn't say anything but pressed a little harder on the accelerator. The Cavalier's engine moaned and the car sped up. The punks in the truck were gaining on them, though. They had one thing on their mind: revenge. They'd been embarrassed, shamed, and they now had to regain their honor and prove at least to themselves and each other that they were the men they thought they were.

"We need to end this here and now," Jed said. He'd known punks like the ones in the truck behind him and more than once had been the brunt of their efforts to humiliate. They wouldn't give up until they satisfied their need to not only save face but to reestablish themselves as the dominant males.

"You gonna stop the car and go all Jackie Chan on them?"

He wanted to, but taking on three guys in the middle of the road was different than when they were stuck behind a table. The odds would be against him. "Nope. I have something else in mind."

He took his foot off the accelerator and allowed the car to slow.

"So you're inviting a conflict but not Jackie Chan style."

"Sort of." He glanced in the mirror. The truck was no more than twenty feet off his rear bumper. "I can't do anything unless they show aggression. Right now, they're just tailing us. Nothing illegal about that."

As if the punks in the truck had somehow heard him, the truck suddenly lurched forward and tapped the rear bumper of the Cavalier.

"That's what I was waiting for," Jed said.

Karen grabbed her seat belt and clicked it into place. "They're nuts."

"They're more than that. Listen to me: things are going to get really rough if I don't end this right now. Are you okay with that?"

"Do I have a choice?"

"You always have a choice. Say you're not okay, and I'll find another way."

The truck rammed the Cavalier again. The car's tires squealed and skidded, the tail end swerved right and left.

"Do what you have to do."

"Do you trust me?"

"I don't even know you." She paused, turned and glanced at the goons in the truck. "But yes, I do."

All three of the punks were in the front seat of the truck. Goldilocks drove, Buzzcut was in the middle, Mohawk rode shotgun. None of them wore seat belts.

Jed reached over his left shoulder and grabbed the seat belt, locked it into place. He looked to Karen then checked the mirror again. "Hang on."

He punched the accelerator and the Cavalier lunged forward, putting distance between it and the truck. But the truck responded in kind and was soon less than ten feet from the car's bumper again.

Jed tapped the brake, causing the truck to respond by slowing, then he stomped on the gas and pushed the pedal to the floor. The Cavalier raced forward, reaching a speed of nearly seventy miles per hour. The truck was a good fifty yards behind them, struggling to keep the same rate of acceleration.

"Here we go," Jed said.

"I was afraid you were going to say that."

Jed tapped the brake again and yanked the steering wheel to the left. As soon as the front of the car began the turn he yanked up on the handbrake. The back end of the Cavalier skidded in a half-circle. When the car had spun a complete one-eighty, Jed straightened the wheel and released the handbrake. The Cavalier sat in the road facing the oncoming truck.

Karen screamed.

The truck closed the distance in a mere second.

Jed flinched.

At the last possible moment, the truck's brakes locked and it swerved to the right. It skidded across the shoulder, bounced into a shallow gully that ran along the road, and came to an abrupt stop.

Jed sucked in a deep breath and blew it out.

Next to him, Karen opened her mouth but didn't say anything. Finally, she said, "Are you gonna go?"

"Not yet," Jed said. He wanted to make sure there was movement in the truck's cab before he took off. The punks should be banged up but with no serious injuries. Behind the wheel of the truck, Goldilocks sat back in the seat, put his hand to his nose, then thumped the steering wheel with two open palms.

"Okay, let's go." Jed hit the gas on the Cavalier and turned the car around.

After a minute of silent driving, Karen said, "I probably don't have to tell you this, but you're as nuts as they are."

"Not nuts," Jed said. "It was the only way. They would have never given up."

"How old are you anyway?"

"Eighteen."

"Where'd you learn how to do that spinny thing?"

Jed paused for a moment. He checked the mirrors. "Where are we going?"

"You're driving. Where are you taking me?"

"Where's home?"

Karen pointed ahead. "Next road on the left. You didn't answer my question."

"The spinny thing."

"Yes."

"When you spend your life getting bounced from foster home to foster home you have a lot of free time to goof off."

"So you're not a nut, but you're a goof?"

"Something like that."

"And what comes next for you?"

He glanced at her. "After I drop you off?"

"After high school."

"I'm joining the Army."

"Infantry?"

"Rangers."

"You gonna beat people up in diners and do spinny things for them?"

Jed smiled. "Something like that." He checked the mirrors again. "You gotta be kidding me."

Behind them, a hundred yards back, the truck swerved in its lane. The front bumper sat cockeyed like a crooked toothless grin. The grill was twisted and bent, turning the grin into more of a grimace. Karen swiveled in her seat and groaned. "Seriously?"

Jed sighed. "They're not going to give up."

He hit the brakes and the Cavalier skidded to a stop.

"What are you doing?" Karen said.

The truck slowed and stopped behind them, twenty feet away.

"There's only one way to deal with jerks like this." He opened his door.

Karen grabbed his arm. "Wait. What makes you an expert at dealing with jerks?"

"I know the type. Not every foster dad is a loving one."

"What if they have a gun?"

Jed glanced in the mirror. Goldilocks sat behind the wheel. Blood darkened the lower half of his face. Beside him, Buzzcut jabbered on about something. He, too, had blood smeared across his chin and cheek. Mohawk leaned against the window, his nose swollen and red as a tomato. "They don't seem like the type."

Jed stepped out of the car and headed in the direction of the truck. The driver's side door opened and Goldilocks stumbled out, obviously shaken from the collision with the gully and unsteady on his legs.

A string of curses spilled from Goldilock's mouth. He headed toward Jed, fire in his eyes, fists clenched. Jed approached him straight on. When they were no more than five feet apart, Goldilocks lunged at Jed and swung a haymaker that Jed easily dodged. With Goldilocks off balance, Jed grabbed a handful of his shirt and swung him around. The punk nearly fell and would have if Jed hadn't held him up. Jed could have messed up his face even more, broken a few teeth. He could have taught Goldilocks a lesson the jerk would never forget. But he didn't. Instead he yanked him around and took a hold of the shirt at the back of Goldilock's neck. He then walked the troublemaker back to the truck and threw him against the hood. Inside the cab, Mohawk still leaned against the window. Buzzcut watched with bulging eyes.

With Goldilocks pinned to the hood of the truck, Jed leaned over him. "You need to get yourself and your friends to a hospital."

Goldilocks cursed and tried to wriggle his way free of Jed's grip.

"Seriously, man. You're hurt. Your friends are hurt. Get some help. We can finish this later if you want."

"I'm gonna kill you, man."

From inside the truck's cab, Buzzcut yelled, "Let him go, dude. It's over."

"If you want to finish this," Jed said to Goldilocks, "I'm ready when you are. But I'd suggest you just let this go. Forget about it."

Goldilocks continued to struggle but he was no match for Jed, who easily held him against the truck. "I'm gonna kill you. And your chick, too."

Jed tightened his grip on Goldilocks's shirt and leaned closer. "That's your choice to try, but I'm warning you now: you touch her and I'll mess you up so bad your mother won't even recognize you." He released Goldilocks but stood over him. "Get yourself patched up. Your friends look like they could use some help too."

Jed turned and walked back to the Cavalier. With his back to Goldilocks he watched Karen's eyes for any sign that the punk would try to surprise him from behind. He didn't. In the Cavalier, with the doors closed and locked, Jed looked at Karen and forced a smile.

"You're shaking," she said.

"I don't like confrontation."

"Could have fooled me."

Jed worked the gear shift and drove the car away from the scene.

"You think they'll come after you?"

"I don't think so." He glanced at her, then back to the road. "You may want to find a new job, though."

"Will I see you again?"

"You said I was nuts. You always hang around with nutjobs?"

"You said you were a goof. Nuts scare me; goofs are entertaining."

"I see. Then in that case I think you will see me again."

"Good." She sat back in her seat and smiled.

APPENDIX:

10 SIMPLE WAYS TO IMPROVE YOUR FICTION WRITING

1. Get in the habit of being observant.

    Watch people. Watch how they move, stand, talk, what they do with their hands, how they walk. Take not of their posture and body language. Be aware of your surroundings. Look at landscapes and cityscapes. Take note of architecture and kinds of trees. Notice the details of everyday life around you. Flower petals, tree bark, the way trees move in the wind. Clouds. Roadways. Keep your eyes open and learn to really observe.

2. Listen when people talk.

    Take note of not only what they say but how they say it. Words they use. Voice inflections. Non-verbal communication. Listen to the rhythm of conversations. Train your ears to not only hear but to listen.

3. Get comfortable with asking lots of questions.

    Ask people about their family, their history, their job, their likes and dislikes. Be inquisitive and curious. There's no such thing as a dumb question.

4. Read in a variety of genres and read to learn, not just to be entertained.

When you read, read to learn. Watch for how the author develops the characters. Take note of the pacing of the story. Note how dialogue is written. How settings are described. How action is described. Read with an eye to study and learn.

5. Write. Practice, practice, practice.

   There's no shame in writing garbage. There's no shame in writing pieces no one will ever read. Think of it this way. Pianists play for hours and hours when no one is listening. It's called practice. Writers must practice as well. Writing well is not easy and takes time and practice. Give yourself space to grow and hone your craft.

6. Sharpen and strengthen your imagination.

   Learn the art of imagining. Make up stories in your head. Let your imagination run wild. Read very imaginative books and watch imaginative movies. Always be thinking and creating in your mind.

7. Find what inspires you and make note of it.

   Different things inspire different people in different ways. Find what inspires you. Is it the writing of a certain author? Is it a certain type of music? A song in particular? Is it a walk in nature? Being by the ocean? Whatever it is try to capture that and relive it to inspire yourself. You don't have to be "inspired" to write but it sure helps!

8. Allow yourself the freedom to express.

   This goes along with imagination and practice. Play around with words and stories. Create freely even if you think the writing will never amount to anything. You never know. And the process of creating, of expressing, will pay huge dividends in your ability to write fiction well.

9. Get comfortable being vulnerable.

    Be okay with showing your wounds to readers, with expressing those deepest, darkest secrets you hide. The best fiction comes from a place of vulnerability and genuineness that we usually don't see or feel in everyday life. It resonates with readers because we all feel it but rarely express it. Tap into those raw emotions you let few people see and pour them onto the page.

10. Look for story ideas in everyday life.

    The basic foundation of all stories is real people dealing with real problems. We see that every day in the world around us. Pay attention. Watch. Listen. Learn. View every interaction with someone else as a potential story. Every news event. Every headline. They are all potential stories, or scenes within a story, or characters to populate your stories. Fiction is the stuff of life and life happens all around us all the time.

TYPES OF FICTION

Fiction comes in all shapes and sizes. And lengths. For your reference, here is a list of types of fiction and their general word counts. Please note, these numbers are very general and will vary depending on which source you pull them from.

Flash fiction: 50-1,000 words

Short story: 1,000-12,000 words

Novelette: 12,000-20,000 words

Novella: 20,000-40,000 words

Novel: 40,000+ words

Now, again, generally speaking, word length will vary depending on the genre. Young adult books may range from 40,000 to 80,000 words, romance may range from 50,000 to 100,000 words, and suspense may fall between 80,000 and 100,000 words. This is very general and you will find lots of variations in word count. If you're serious about writing a novel and submitting it for publication your best bet is to do some research and either find out what publishers are looking for or, if you're going to self-publish, research what word counts are most popular in your given genre. But don't get hung up on word count. Readers rarely mind how long a book or short story is as long as the story is good and the price is appropriate.

GENRES OF FICTION

Fiction comes in all shapes and sizes. I've already included a guide for the varying lengths of fiction. Here is a link to an article that covers the different genres. A genre is basically what type of story is being told. Is it adventure? Suspense? Romance? Historical? Mystery? Is it geared toward women readers? Young adults?

Writer's Digest University: "Definitions of Fiction Categories and Genres" http://resources.writersonlineworkshops.com/resources/definitions-of-fiction-categories-and-genres/

What genre you decided to write in depends a lot on what you enjoy to read. If you love adventure stories, I would suggest writing an adventure novel or short story. If you love to read romance, write romance. Write what you love.

One last note on genres. I would suggest reading in a wide variety of genres. It will be very beneficial for you to understand how the genres work and to get comfortable with the differing styles of writing.

COMMON MISTAKES TO AVOID

Head-hopping

Remember, one POV character per scene (yes, a scene can be an entire chapter or a scene within a chapter). Determine which character will get the POV for the scene then stay in that character's POV only.

Not staying in POV

POV is all about seeing and experiencing the world through a character's eyes and mind. If he can't see it, don't write it. If he can't know it, don't write it. If he can't taste, smell, hear, or feel it, don't write it.

Passive writing

This is a complicated matter, passive vs. active writing. The easiest way it can be explained is with the word "was". Let's get real simple. Here's the difference in a nutshell. In passive writing the action is being done to the subject which usually results in the word "was" unnecessarily used. In active writing the subject is doing the action.

For instance:

The ball was thrown by Billy. (Passive)

Billy threw the ball. (Active)

Joe was walking down the sidewalk. (Passive)

Joe walked down the sidewalk. (Active).

Be care of "was/-ing" combinations, they are a sure sign of passive writing.

Weak beginnings

The first chapter of any story is the most important. You need to get the first chapter right. And the first paragraph, even the first sentence of that first chapter is critical to grabbing the reader's attention. The first chapter should grab the reader by the shirt collar and not let go. It needs to say, "You need to keep reading to find out what happens." The first chapter should raise questions that will later be answered, it should create suspense and mystery.

Generally speaking, do not include any back story in the first chapter. You want it to grab the reader immediately and move the story forward. There will be time for back story later, the first chapter is a time for forward motion and the creation of a sense of mystery and intrigue.

Telling, not showing

One of the all-time great mantras in fiction writing is "show, don't tell." And it's one of the biggest mistakes novice writers make. They tell us Claire was mad but don't show us her anger. They tell us Diane was bashful but don't show us her shyness. You want to get in the habit of showing the reader what is happening, not merely telling the reader what happened.

For instance:

Jack was mad. (Telling)
Jack balled his fists and clenched his jaw. (Showing)

Andrea felt off-balance. (Telling)

Andrea stumbled to her left and caught herself on the table. The room rotated around her like she was on the inside of a spinning top. (Showing)

See the difference? It's huge. Showing pulls the reader in, makes him part of the action, part of the scene. Telling leaves the reader outside to merely watch from the sidewalk. Showing involves the reader; telling makes the reader a spectator.

SUGGESTED READING

Please note, these novels are strictly suggestions. You may read whatever books you want to read. My only suggestion is to read to learn. As you read, pay attention to the things you've learned in this course and how the author implements them in his or her story.

My suggestion to enhance this course and have it fulfill the requirements for a 1-credit high school class is to read at least five novels.

White Fang by Jack London

Call of the Wild by Jack London

Pride and Prejudice by Jane Austen

The Giver by Lois Lowry

The Citadel by A. J. Cronin

A Pocketful of Rye by A. J. Cronin

Jane Eyre by Charlotte Bronte

Fear Mountain by Mike Dellosso

A Thousand Sleepless Nights by Michael King

The Sign of the Beaver by Elizabeth George Speare

River Rising by Athol Dickson

Winter Haven by Athol Dickson

FINAL PROJECT

Okay, final project time. Your final writing project is to write a short story of at least 5,000 words (double-spaced, 1" margins, font size 12, if typing). You can write in any genre you want but a few guidelines must be adhered to. One, your story must include at least two characters. You can, of course, have more than two. Two, there must be dialogue in your story. And three, there must be a beginning, middle, and end (keep in mind the four stages of a plot arc).

Just a note on short story writing: Due to limited space few short stories include back story about the characters. Other than that, you can use all the techniques you've learned in this course to make your short story as captivating as it can be.

Other than that, have fun! Remember to include what you learned about plot, description, dialogue, characters, and point-of-view. Feel free to use whatever point-of-view and tense you feel the story needs.

PARENTS: If you would like me to grade your child's final project I will make myself available to do so for a $50 fee. The fee includes critiquing an early draft and grading the final draft. If you would like me to grade all the writing assignments and give your child a final grade for the class it is an additional $100 fee. If interested in this, please contact me at mikedellosso6797@gmail.com.

About the author . . .

Mike Dellosso is the author of a dozen novels. Under his real name he writes suspense/thrillers and under the pseudonym Michael King he writes contemporary fiction. He has also written numerous articles for magazines, websites, blogs, and newsletters. Mike is a popular conference speaker and teacher and an adjunct professor of creative writing.

Mike is a colon cancer survivor and a lifelong stutterer who discovered that writing helped him overcome his speech impediment. He has been writing novels since 2005.

Mike and his wife have five daughters and live in southern Pennsylvania. They homeschool all their children.

You can learn more about Mike and his books at his website, www.mikedellossobooks.com, on Facebook, www.facebook.com/mikedellosso, or on Goodreads. His books are available wherever books are sold, online and otherwise.

www.ingramcontent.com/pod-product-compliance
Lightning Source LLC
Chambersburg PA
CBHW080324290526
45793CB00006B/1197